Building Thriving School Communities Focused on Wellness and Equity by Leveraging MTSS

Keep supporting Kids!

Lori Lynass

Building Thriving School Communities Focused on Wellness and Equity by Leveraging MTSS

Lori Lynass, Bridget Walker, and Erika McDowell

ROWMAN & LITTLEFIELD
Lanham • Boulder • New York • London

Published by Rowman & Littlefield
An imprint of The Rowman & Littlefield Publishing Group, Inc.
4501 Forbes Boulevard, Suite 200, Lanham, Maryland 20706
www.rowman.com

86-90 Paul Street, London EC2A 4NE

British Library Cataloguing in Publication Information Available

Library of Congress Cataloging-in-Publication Data

Names: Lynass, Lori, author. | Walker, Bridget, author. | McDowell, Erika, author.
Title: Building thriving school communities focused on wellness and equity by
    leveraging MTSS / Lori Lynass, Bridget Walker, and Erika McDowell.
Description: Lanham, Maryland : Rowman & Littlefield, 2024. | Includes bibliographical
    references.
Identifiers: LCCN 2024005892 (print) | LCCN 2024005893 (ebook) | ISBN
    9781475874358 (cloth) | ISBN 9781475874365 (paperback) | ISBN
    9781475874372 (ebook)
Subjects: LCSH: Multi-tiered systems of support (Education). | Affective education. |
    School environment. | Students--Mental health. | Well-being.
Classification: LCC LB1029.M85 L96 2024 (print) | LCC LB1029.M85 (ebook) | DDC
    370.15/34–dc23/eng/20240307
LC record available at https://lccn.loc.gov/2024005892
LC ebook record available at https://lccn.loc.gov/2024005893

♾️™ The paper used in this publication meets the minimum requirements of American
National Standard for Information Sciences—Permanence of Paper for Printed Library
Materials, ANSI/NISO Z39.48-1992.

This book is dedicated to my husband Jeff and my two children Ole and Scout. Their relentless patience, support and cheerleading made this book a reality. "We work hard and we play hard."

—Lori Lynass

To the first teachers I ever had, my beloved parents, Warren and Mary McDowell. I would not be the educator I am today without your love and guidance. You have shown how "being the greatest tool in your toolbox" can change and impact lives. Thank you for supporting all learners, especially me.

—Erika McDowell

To my family. who gave me a solid foundation and a boundless love for learning, and to my husband Scott, who has supported me every step of the way. Also, to all my students over the years, who have taught me so much. Thank you.

—Bridget Walker

Contents

Statements from the Authors

I have always held a deep passion for supporting youth, especially youth with intensive behavioral needs. I was inspired to pursue my doctorate as a special education teacher who knew there had to be a way to prevent many of the youth I was teaching from needing such intensive support. I knew the change was beyond my classroom and driven by the larger need for a more effective system. It was during my post-doctorate work that I first heard about the Positive Behavioral Interventions and Supports (PBIS) framework, which was a new concept. I had the privilege to be mentored by Dr. Douglas Cheney, professor emeritus for the University of Washington, who was a pioneer of this work. I knew that this three-tiered approach could help schools to better organize their systems and practices and gain better outcomes for all students.

The increasing impacts we have seen related to stress and trauma that were catapulted forward during COVID-19 inspired me to want to share my knowledge about Multi-Tiered System of Supports (MTSS) and its role in supporting school wellness in this book. I feel that when done with fidelity and with a strong focus on equity, MTSS can help transform schools into effectively delivering academics while also centering wellness and community. It is this focus on wellness and community that so many schools lack. When schools lack this focus, they are not educating the whole child. This focus on wellness and community also benefits our dedicated school staff. The lack of support for staff wellness during COVID drove many staff to leave the field of education.

Focusing on the leader and leadership teams only makes sense since they play a pivotal role in driving the climate of a school or district. Having personally been in more than 2,000 schools, I can tell you that an effective leader is essential. Most leaders I have had the honor to work with strive to best serve their students and their staff, but they need tools that can help them be successful. This book is for you! I hope you can go forth and continue the good work of supporting our most treasured assets, the children and youth of our nation.

—Lori Lynass

The great writer and social justice activist James Baldwin wrote, "not everything that is faced can be changed, but nothing can be changed until it is faced." Public education in America is facing a reckoning that must be faced, so that it can be transformed. The traditional, nineteenth century, industrial model of education no longer meets the needs of our children, our educators, our families, or our communities. Too many are excluded, disenfranchised, and left behind. The structures and schedules are outmoded and inefficient.

As a veteran educator, I have watched as the same dialogues, culture wars and pedagogical arguments are recycled across decades, while little has changed in terms of student outcomes and well-being. Schools remain deeply underfunded, educators continue to be underpaid and overworked, and principals are charged with creating miracles with limited resources and support. We must stop pretending that schools as they have been traditionally structured are up to meeting the needs of today's students and families. Once we accept this, we can get on with the critical work of building our schools for twenty-first century.

Our goal with this book is to anchor key approaches and practices that are evidence based, inclusive, and equitable in a way that helps schools and districts build a sustainable approach to school transformation. There is essential work that is necessary to meet the needs of our *all* of our current and future students and the educators who support them. The good news is that the practices we explore here are shown to make a difference in the real world of diverse schools and communities across the country. It is work that takes time and requires change for all involved, but it pays off.

In teacher education there is a saying that we must "attend to Maslow before Bloom." That is to say that we must make sure the basic needs of our students, families and education professionals are met, before we can expect academic growth and development. The approaches we explore in this book address both creating a learning community that supports our learners' well-being *and* builds the cognitive and social-emotional skills needed for learning and development. This is our hope and path toward the future.

As the visionary Maya Angelou said, "I did then what I knew how to do. Now that I know better, I do better." Together, we can and must do better—for our students and for one another.

—Bridget Walker

I'm sick and tired of being sick and tired.—Fannie Lou Hamer

I know you are. It is clear in various articles/books targeted to educators. I am sick and tired and should probably get some of this sleep people are experiencing that I cannot. Currently, I use captioning services if I really want to write, but my jaw is aching tremendously like someone has gone three rounds on my face. Yes, I have trauma. But no one has physically hit me. I, who uses she/her/Dr., have never been in a fight—something I actually shared with my learners. I was and still am proud of that. To address significant issues in schools, we must embrace love, at all times, and adapt, by any means necessary.

It is life or death, for all of us. *How are you?* This question has been asked of me for weeks at this point. I am not okay. As I have flown and driven to different schools, districts, conferences, offices, hotels, churches, and even prisons, I have come to the stark realization that it isn't just me. *We* are not okay. I know a little about grind culture, I identify as a woman with lots of jobs, and I am currently either pausing, on leave, or on an accommodation plan. She/her/Dr. E knows about the grind because her cute pink orthodontic is currently clinching, culture wars are raging, and a whole lack of love is lacking in our educational environments. We, as a global educational community, are not okay.

I love Dr. Cassandra Brene Brown. She has a great video that talks about the power of vulnerability. I met her work through the marketing tour for book with Tarana Burke, You Are Your Best Thing: *Vulnerability, Shame Resilience, and the Black Experience.* What I love about their work is the discussion on how belonging is a vulnerable act. Brown says, "Vulnerability is not knowing the outcome but doing it anyway because it's the brave thing to do." So I rest as an act of resistance. I am being vulnerable and allowing my community to stand in solidarity against the forces that want my human spirit to physically, mentally, emotionally, and spiritually break. I'm being extremely vulnerable for our collective healing and community.

Let us not just play oppression Olympics but have courageous conversations with each other to feel it to heal it and not repeat history again. We *can* be okay. But, unless we really talk about the lack of love and belonging in our educational systems, we will be reproducing oppressive environments for the communities we serve. This lack of love can cause learners and the folx that serve them, to disassociate themselves from practices and position themselves as not belonging to spaces of learning. This is a call for all of us to lean into a pedagogy of love and belonging, even though it may be difficult for you as a practitioner. Floyd Cobb and John Krownapple, co-authors of Belonging Through a Culture of Dignity: The Keys to Successful Equity Implementation, define *belonging* as experiencing appreciation, validation, acceptance, and fair treatment within an environment. You see the community as they are and curate environments where all of our learners and partners will thrive, including you. There is a pedagogy of love, community, and belonging that we are missing. Let us move toward a healing pedagogy of communicative belonging.

—Erika McDowell

Foreword

Kent McIntosh

It shouldn't be news to anyone that our educational systems are in crisis. Educators today are faced with deepening attacks on the profession, unprecedented turnover, and an escalating mental health crisis exacerbated by the COVID-19 pandemic. Moreover, debates about how (or even whether) to acknowledge and ameliorate racial disparities in educational outcomes have often led to no changes, a preservation of the status quo that continues to perpetuate those disparities.

Crisis, however, is not new to educators. We are used to all sorts of crises, even if the current ones feel especially challenging to address. So what do we need to improve education for both students and educators? Is it another program, curriculum, or technology that promises to solve all of our problems? No, we don't need another shiny new thing to be told to implement, but we do need systems to support us in doing the things we know we need to do. We need a framework, a way to organize the supports we provide to students, as well as to each other. That framework is Multi-Tiered System of Supports (MTSS).

As the authors describe in the chapters that follow, MTSS has proven effectiveness. Put simply, if you want an innovation to be fully implemented and sustained, implement it within the systems, data, and practices of an MTSS. Hold yourself to the plan by measuring fidelity of implementation. We are seeing emerging research that those school and district teams that have embraced MTSS as a way of work are seeing vastly improved outcomes, even with the crises that we've seen in education as of late.

But like the steel skeletons of buildings, a framework like MTSS can look cold and rigid. How do we make MTSS come to life? We fill it with the things that will bring us the outcomes we value. We expand what people have typically considered to fit within the framework, deftly avoiding the behavior wars that say there's only one way to support student development. We consider the recipients of the framework, especially those who have been least likely to benefit from it. We make it feel like home to our students and families, so they can bring their authentic selves inside. Moreover, we give them the tools to co-construct the framework alongside us.

We use MTSS to make our schools places where joy can happen. That is how to make a framework come alive.

Kent McIntosh is director of the National Technical Assistance Center on Positive Behavioral Interventions and Supports (PBIS*)*.

Acknowledgments

I want to first acknowledge my two co-authors, Bridget Walker and Erika McDowell. Bridget has been with me on this whole journey, and I would not have engaged in this book without her willingness to collaborate. To Erika, who then agreed to join this wild ride and brought a needed lens to our focus on equity. To my family, my parents who have always been so proud of every small accomplishment and make me feel like I can take on anything I set my mind to. To my husband, who often shakes his head when I take on big goals such as this, but whom is my biggest supporter. To my children, who never stop encouraging me and remind me that this work is truly about making schools better for the youth.

—Lori Lynass

This work is the product of collaboration and community! My heartfelt thanks to my co-authors, Lori and Erika. They are both brilliant and brought life to our ideas!

—Bridget Walker

I acknowledge and give thanks to the land and environments on which we live and work, and to the ancestors who come before us. This book would not have been birthed without my loves, Bridget and Lori. I know you love the work we do. I hope that this love is felt by every reader.

—Erika McDowell

Collectively, we would like to thank the many educators and experts who have supported our work over the years and whose experiences and insights helped make this book possible.

Our thanks to Johnny Phu at the Lake Washington School District in Redmond, Washington and Cheri Simpson, Todd Wehmeyer, Christy Kehr, Nathaniel Hoston, Deron Woods, and Desirae Monzingo at Kent School District in Kent, Washington for being willing to be interviewed for the vignettes in this book and for being so wonderful to collaborate with for so many years.

To Kent McIntosh, Director of the National Technical Assistance Center on Positive Behavioral Interventions and Supports (PBIS), who has been a colleague, cheerleader, and champion for our work over many years.

We are also grateful to the support of the Association of Positive Behavior Interventions and Supports and our many mentors and colleagues there, including Kathleen Lane, Lucille Eber, Rob Horner, George Sugai, and many others. We especially want to call out the equity champions Naomi Brahim, Nikole Hollins-Sims, Rhonda Neese, and Clynita Grafeenreed. Thanks also to our colleagues and supporters at the Northwest PBIS Network, including Jessica Swain-Bradway. They keep the work growing and going!

Of course, we are indebted to the many teachers, administrators, district, and state leaders who we have worked with and learned from over the years. You kept us honest and grounded in the reality of schools today, and your dedication to making a difference for students, staff, and families has been inspirational.

Lastly, to our friend and mentor Doug Cheney, who first introduced us to the tiered systems of support framework and taught us so much over the years. His wisdom, support, and generosity made this work possible.

—Lori Lynass and Bridget Walker

Introduction

MTSS FOCUSED ON EQUITY AND WELLNESS

Prior to the COVID-19 pandemic, schools in the United States were already facing the challenges of supporting a rising number of health issues presented by students. Since the pandemic, the increased demand for behavioral, mental health, and social-emotional needs in addition to academic needs has overwhelmed schools and school leaders. Yet, it is the schools' professional responsibility to ensure each student learns, grows, and feels a sense of belonging. To meet these rising challenges, it can be tempting for leaders to look for quick-fix programs to plug into place. What is needed instead is to build a Multi-Tiered System of Supports (MTSS) that focuses on wellness and engages the families and communities that schools serve.

THE MTSS FRAMEWORK AS A RECIPE

In this book, the discussion of MTSS builds upon the definition of MTSS offered by Freeman et al. (2017), "MTSS is an overarching referent for frameworks designed to target academic and behavioral challenges with a focus on a tiered continuum of evidence-based practices within the context of prevention science and implementation research." Chapter 1 explores the history of and theory behind MTSS and breaks down its major components.

It is important to note that MTSS is a framework and not a package program. This framework is designed to be adapted by the user to adjust it for the cultural and contextual uniqueness of their school. Frameworks can define the work and skills, shared in a manner where all school partners/participants are welcome and included in safe environments, and they create a world in which all can thrive.

One can think of frameworks as recipes that can be adapted by school leaders to meet the needs of *all* for quality education. Eating and education are both universal needs. The creative and conscientious host gathers information about guests to plan a nutritious meal that will meet the guests' needs. Similarly, school leaders can gather data to adapt MTSS frameworks to meet the behavioral, emotional, cultural, and academic needs of *all* in their classrooms in an environment that promotes learning, inclusiveness, and safety for all students.

What is your recipe for implementation of MTSS in your school? What data are you using to make the MTSS framework equitable and culturally responsive? In a recipe for a successful MTSS that truly creates wellness and community, all schools need these base ingredients:

- equity
- connectedness
- inclusivity
- culturally responsive pedagogy

Figure I.1 captures these ingredients in creating schools focused on wellness and healthy systems in which all can thrive.

Because educators' actions and practices are critical in helping learners, they must use strategic tools to assist the implementation of MTSS to ensure it is equitable, full of love, centered in evidence-based practice, and understands the history of its community and education. Tools in this book and others (e.g., Hollins-Sims et al., 2022) can assist schools to become more culturally and contextually responsive to student needs and to highlight contributing factors to disproportionality.

Recipe for MTSS Focused on Wellness and Community

Main Ingredients:

- **Culturally Responsive Pedagogy:** facilitates relevant learning opportunities
- **Connectedness:** facilitates positive community culture
- **Equity:** facilitates access
- **Inclusivity:** facilitates belonging

*While these ingredients are not necessarily equal parts, make sure that each of them feels balanced in your recipe. Add other ingredients as needed for your school or district.

Figure I.1.   Recipe of Critical Ingredients to Build Wellness with MTSS.

Building MTSS allows leaders to dismantle systems of oppression that are showing up in school districts across our nation. This book will also assist leaders to build what Bell Hooks describes as "a community of resistance" letting leaders know that they are not alone in implementing MTSS.

HOW TO USE THIS BOOK

The chapters in this book are designed to be read in the order they appear. Content in subsequent chapters builds on the previous chapters. If readers are already implementing MTSS they may move through the content in various order. Most chapters conclude with a table suggesting ways that leaders can use implementation science to increase the fidelity and outcomes of their MTSS framework.

REFERENCES

Freeman, J., Sugai, G., Simonsen, B., & Everett, S. (2017). MTSS coaching: Bridging knowing to doing. *Theory into Practice, 56*, 29–37.

Hollins-Sims, N.Y., Kaurudar, E.J., & Runge, T.J. (2022). *Creating equitable practices in PBIS: Growing a positive school climate for sustainable outcomes* (1st ed.). Routledge.

Chapter 1

Building and Sustaining a Thriving School Community with a Multi-Tiered System of Supports

WHY A FOCUS ON EQUITY AND WELLBEING IN SCHOOLS IS THE FIRST STEP

Any educational leader who has spent time in a school since the COVID-19 pandemic began already knows many of the reasons needed to focus on equity and wellness in schools. While one may think of equity and wellness as separate things, they can be quite intertwined. When students feel physically and emotionally well, they are better prepared to engage in learning. When every student feels safe and connected in their schools, they are more likely to have higher rates of attendance and performance. The same is true for the staff in our schools. Unfortunately, data shows that students and staff have diminished levels of wellness and that the impact is not equitable. Staff and students of color have been disproportionally impacted by the health and economic impacts of the pandemic (CDC, 2023).

In 2023, depression and anxiety were among the leading causes of illness for adolescents (World Health Organization). To kick off Mental Health Awareness Month in May of 2023, the U.S. Surgeon General, Dr. Vivek Murthy, declared loneliness as a new public health epidemic in the United States. Dr. Murthy noted the lack of social connection youth may feel in schools and the detrimental effects it can have on health and wellbeing (Department of Health and Human Services, 2023).

Suicide is one of the leading causes of death for youth in the United States aged 15–19 (WHO, 2023). Nationally, up to 80% of the services that students access for mental health support are provided at school and 35% of students get support exclusively at school. Students who are racially or ethnically diverse or who are living in poverty are even more likely to rely solely on schools for mental health supports (Ali et al., 2019).

Before the COVID-19 pandemic, schools across the United States had already been reporting an uptick in students experiencing trauma, struggling with mental health concerns, and committing suicide. Data shows that one in five children were experiencing negative behavior health outcomes in 2020 (SAMHSA, 2020). The pandemic exacerbated this further, causing increased stress for not only students but also for families and staff. The overall wellness of a school is determined by many factors, including mental health, social-emotional learning (SEL), social determinates of health, students' connection to school, and family and community involvement. These components directly impact the academic outcomes of students in schools, while academic outcomes in turn can directly impact wellness, creating a cycle of ongoing outcomes. It can be overwhelming for a school or district to organize all the initiatives, supports, and programs needed to address the many needs of students and staff. This is why incorporating the framework of the Multi-Tiered System of Supports (MTSS) is necessary. Using MTSS, a school community becomes one that thrives, centering on both equity and wellbeing in schools.

WHAT IS A MULTI-TIERED SYSTEM OF SUPPORTS?

The term *Multi-Tiered System of Supports (MTSS)* may seem like one of the numerous fads in education that also has yet another acronym attached to it. However, the core concepts of MTSS have long existed in the form of evidenced based practices employed by schools. MTSS combines two existing frameworks for support: the Response to Intervention (RTI) model (Fuchs et al., 2003) and the Positive Behavioral Interventions and Supports (PBIS) model (Walker et al., 1996).

The research involving the RTI and PBIS frameworks were initiated after the reauthorization of the Individuals with Disabilities Education Improvement Act (IDEIA, 2004) and the No Child Left Behind Act (NCLB, 2001). Both acts emphasize the use of scientifically based research and practices to improve the academic and behavioral outcomes of students, which is a core focus of both RTI and PBIS. The 2015 the reauthorization of NCLB, called the Every Student Succeeds Act (ESSA), included specific language about integrating the supports developed within RTI and PBIS into what became known as a comprehensive multi-tiered system of support.

To date, no other comprehensive school reform approach has had the staying power of RTI and PBIS. In fact, the National Center for PBIS, which was established in 1998, has received the longest consistent amount of funding from the Department of Education (www.pbis.org). In 2019, the Integrated Multi-Tiered Systems of Support (I-MTSS) Research Network was funded by the Institute for Education Sciences to study how to better integrate academics, social-emotional, and behavioral supports using the MTSS framework (2023).

The advantage of combining these two frameworks into one is simple: academic skills and behavior skills are closely connected. There is ample research demonstrating that if a child has a deficit in behavioral or social-emotional skills, they are more likely than their peers to have or to later develop deficits in academics (Nelson et al., 2013). Using a three-tiered approach, MTSS enables schools to organize a continuum of practices and services for all students that starts with prevention. The main goals of MTSS focus on prevention and early access to support. The core features of MTSS are:

- Employing evidenced practices
- Using data-based decision-making
- Having team-driven shared leadership
- Using a structured continuum of supports
- Keeping an intentional focus on equity
- Fostering authentic student, family, and community engagement
- Placing an emphasis implementation fidelity

The core features of the list can be summarized with the words equity, inclusion, data, systems, and practices. MTSS provides a framework for schools and districts to use to organize all the initiatives and systems necessary for greater efficiency and effectiveness with a focus on high outcomes for all students and families. Figure 1.1 from the National PBIS Technical Assistance Center shows the relationship of these elements working together.

Whether one begins this work by focusing on behavior or academics, these core features remain central to successful implementation. The MTSS framework prompts schools to shift away from a focus on how to change or "fix" the student to a focus on how to change the environment and the approaches of adults to bring about the desired student growth.

Looking at figure 1.1, the interchange between practices, systems, and data is evident. At the school level, data is used to decide which practices may be needed for the students in that school to experience the highest possible outcomes. A systems-based approach is then used to ensure that the student is receiving or accessing the practices a school has chosen. The outcomes of the practice are monitored to measure growth or change. If a team is not seeing the desired growth, they question whether the system is supporting the

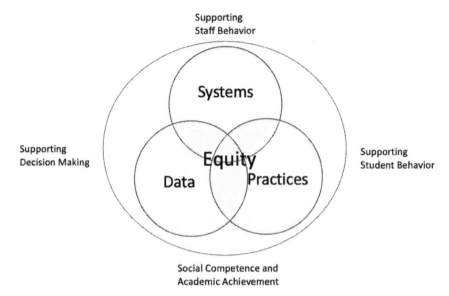

Figure 1.1.   Core Features of Multi-Tiered Systems of Support, Center on PBIS (2023).

practice to be delivered with fidelity. If yes, then it is the practice that may need to change.

UNDERSTANDING THE THREE TIERS OF MTSS

Borrowing from the RTI and PBIS frameworks, the MTSS framework organizes supports across three tiers that are most often represented with a visual of a triangle (see figure 1.2). Rather than students fitting into tiers of support, their needs are addressed in the tiers provided. MTSS is intended to address student needs through a coherent framework that incorporates a whole-child approach that supports both the academic skills and the social-emotional skills. Included in this framework are related supports such as mental health, family supports, and transitional supports.

In the first tier of the three-tiered model, the focus is on building universal supports for all staff, students, and families. This is done by providing high-quality universal instruction for social, emotional, behavioral, and academic needs. Federal guidance through NCLB and IDEIA are responsible for the emphasis placed on appropriate instruction being delivered in the classroom and the accountability of schools to provide that instruction using scientifically based practices (Williams, 2015).

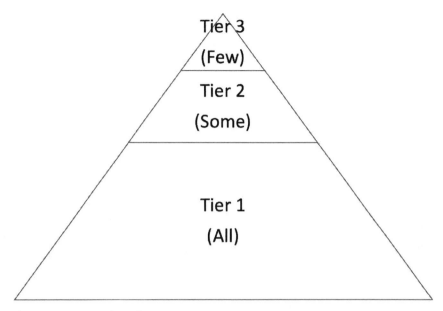

Figure 1.2.   MTSS Tiers of Support, Center on PBIS (2023).

Brown-Chidsey and Steege (2005) remind us that Tier 1 both "starts and ends in the general education classroom." When implemented with fidelity, a district should have data that indicates an average of 80–90% of students responding to Tier 1. Schools are encouraged to start implementation at Tier 1 to prevent more students from needing to access the supports provided in tiers 2 and 3. Academically, this is building solid core instruction across all content areas. Instruction at Tier 1 should be explicit and differentiated but also include flexible grouping that promotes active student engagement.

Tier 2 provides increased supports and strategies to some students who need more support than the Tier 1 system is currently providing them. In general, students access a Tier 2 support for about 6–10 weeks and often in a small group-based format so students can be served more efficiently. For academics, this is done in the classroom. An example would be a reading group for students with similar reading strategy needs. The goal of Tier 2 is to meet needs early and prevent the need for more intensive supports.

According to the Center on PBIS (2023) Tier 2 interventions are:

- Continuously available
- Accessible within 72 hours of referral
- Very low effort by teachers
- Aligned with school-wide systems
- Implemented by all staff/faculty in a school

- Flexible and based on assessment
- Allocated adequate resources
- Continuously monitored

In Tier 2 students should generally need more adult support and benefit from higher rates of reinforcement or praise, have more time for practicing new skills, and have increased pre-corrections (Center on PBIS, 2023).

Tier 3 provides a layer of intensive individualized supports for a small number (generally 1–5%) of students. Because their needs may be more intensive and longer impacting, students may need to access Tier 3 supports for a longer period of time than in Tier 2. For academic needs, the individualized supports are driven by academic diagnostic data. For behavior, the individualized supports are generally determined by conducting a functional behavioral assessment (FBA) and creating an individualized behavior intervention plan (BIP). A Tier 3 comprehensive functional behavior assessment and implementation guide can be found on the Center on PBIS website (www.pbis.org).

According to McIntosh and Goodman (2016), one common misrule is organizing each tier as a separate system, instead of understanding that the three tiers layer on each other, thus a student may receive supports across each of the tiers. An example of this is a student who only needs Tier 1 for academics but may need to access a Tier 2 or 3 support for social, emotional, or behavioral needs. Using this structure, students can more readily access increased supports when the need arises.

The purposes of MTSS in elementary schools are described by Mellard and Johnson (2008) as threefold: (a) screening and prevention of academic skill deficits, (b) early identification and intervention of students at risk for developing learning problems, and (c) determination of learning disabilities. These purposes represent a primary goal of early identification and intervention of deficits in foundational academic skills. Johnson et al. (2009) stated, "The primary purpose of [MTSS] in secondary is to build the capacity of the school to meet the increasing demands for a diverse student population to meet rigorous standards for graduation."

MTSS AS A TOOL FOR INCREASING EQUITY

MTSS is about creating high-functioning schools that can best serve the needs of all our learners. At the center of a high-functioning school is a focus on equity and wellbeing. The data-based approach in MTSS allows schools to deeply examine systemic racial issues and to prevent the negative outcomes of schooling, which has become predictable for many student groups.

Students of color, those from low-income families, those learning English, and students with disabilities have had more exposure to trauma, higher dropout rates, poorer behavior, and social outcomes such as suspensions and expulsions, and lower academic outcomes than their peers (CDC, 2023). Today, 55% of students are culturally and linguistically diverse (CLD). These students consistently have the lowest academic, social, and behavioral outcomes (Office of Special Education Programs, 2021). Although the student population becomes more diverse, a student's race still remains a significant predictor of academic outcomes, even when controlling for poverty (Anyon et al., 2014; Hopson & Lee, 2011). Many strategies have been put forth to address inequity in education but without success (American Institute of Research, 2021).

MTSS has the potential to address these long-standing equity issues and build a new path forward given the flexibility inherent in the framework. MTSS incorporates foundational practices that can address equity in education using data-based decision-making and evidence-based tiered supports to mitigate and prevent academic and behavioral challenges. Given the pervasiveness of inequitable outcomes, a systemic approach should examine the practices, policies, and procedures that produce unequal outcomes.

Educational inequity must be viewed and understood within the historical backdrop of segregation and long-standing policies that have and continue to uphold unfair treatment of students of color and students with disabilities. Given this history, the outcomes currently produced in schools are largely the result of inequitable systems that have been in place for decades. Addressing equity and inclusion must be the overarching goal of systemic change done in collaboration with existing frameworks, such as MTSS.

THE IMPORTANCE AND ROLE OF LEADERSHIP IN BUILDING A HEALTHY COMMUNITY WITH MTSS

Strong leadership that can engage school staff and the larger community in efforts to implement a shared vision for MTSS is essential. Leadership may include district leaders, building administrators, teacher-leaders and instructional specialists, and school-based leadership teams and can ensure that the training, coaching, and resources needed for high-quality implementation are provided. McIntosh and Goodman (2016) suggest these critical features of school and district administrative support for an integrated MTSS model.

- Make public statements of support that are visible to help mobilize all staff.
- Build staff consensus to help keep the initiative moving forward.

- Establish and support school leadership teams.
- Set and maintain district- and school-level standards for implementation.
- Guide the decision-making process by setting ongoing cycles of examining data for decision-making.
- Reinforce leadership team and school faculty by recognizing accomplishments.

Once the MTSS framework has been established, effective leadership plans for and implements continuous activities to improve its efficiency and effectiveness. There are many factors that play into a establishing a high-functioning MTSS system focused on school wellness and equity. As one moves through the implementation process, here are 10 tips that can help leaders build a successful framework:

- Focus on leadership.
- Use an equity-centered team-based approach.
- Involve students, families, and community members from the start.
- Create a shared vision for implementation.
- Use implementation science logic.
- Use data to guide implementation.
- Build capacity within your school or district staff.
- Allocate resources.
- Invest in high-quality training and ongoing coaching.
- Evaluate fidelity and outcomes.

Using this book as a form of a guidebook will help leaders build an MTSS framework that can bring about high-quality results by implementing systems and practices with high fidelity.

EXAMPLE FROM THE FIELD

The Kent School District in Kent, Washington is a mid-sized urban school district serving approximately 25,500 students across 43 schools. The district has been implementing MTSS as a district-wide initiative for the past seven years. When asked them about the factors they have found to be most impactful for building and sustaining MTSS. The factors they replied with are:

- A superintendent who supports MTSS as one of their primary goals and then those leaders who supervise the building principals, sharing that vision.

- A district-level MTSS team representative of the district, schools, families, and community who can support with the MTSS directive.
- Using a yearly district level fidelity tool to measure our implementation.
- High visibility with all our invested parties of our MTSS work.
- A relationships-first approach that takes the time needed to build up trust with all our invested parties.
- The knowledge that we are constantly adapting to meet the buildings where they are; it can't be one size fits all.
- A highly collaborative team of skilled MTSS coaches that meets weekly.

REFERENCES

Ali, M. M., West, K., Teich, J. L., Lynch, S., Mutter, R., & Dubenitz, J. (2019). Utilization of mental health services in educational setting by adolescents in the United States. *Journal of School Health, 89*, 393–401.

American Institute of Research: Center on Multi-tiered System of Supports (2021). *Leveraging MTSS to ensure equitable outcomes.* Retrieved Aug. 30, 2023, from https://mtss4success.org/sites/default/files/2021-07/MTSS_Equity_Brief.pdf.

Anyon, Y., Jenson, J. M., Altschul, I., Farrar, J., McQueen, J., & Greer, E. (2014). The persistent effect of race and the promise of alternatives to suspension in school discipline outcomes. *Children and Youth Service Review, 44*, 379–386.

Brown-Chidsey, R. & Steege, M. (2005). *Response to intervention: Principles and strategies for effective practice.* Guildford Press.

Center for Disease Control and Prevention. (2023). *Youth risk behavior survey system.* Retrieved April 23, 2023. https://www.cdc.gov/healthyyouth/data/yrbs/results.htm.

Center on Positive Behavioral Interventions and Supports (PBIS). (2023). Positive Behavioral Interventions and Supports. www.pbis.org.

Department of Health and Human Services. (2023, May). *New Surgeon General advisory raises alarm about the devastating impact of the epidemic of loneliness and isolation in the United States.* Retrieved May 15, 2023. https://www.hhs.gov/about/news/2023/05/03/new-surgeon-general-advisory-raises-alarm-about-devastating-impact-epidemic-loneliness-isolation-united-states.html.

Fuchs, D., Mock, D., Morgan, P. L., & Young, C. L. (2003). Responsiveness-to-intervention: Definitions, evidence, and implications for the learning disabilities construct. *Learning Disabilities Research and Practice, 18*(3), 157–171.

Hopson, L. M., & Lee, E. (2011). Mitigating the effect of family poverty on academic and behavioral outcomes: The role of school climate in middle and high school. *Children and Youth Services Review, 33*, 2221–2229.

I-MTSS Research Network. (2023). *Brief history of I-MTSS: Summary of major milestones toward an I-MTSS framework.* Integrated Multi-Tiered Systems of Support Research Network, University of Connecticut, www.mtss.org.

Individuals with Disabilities Educational Improvement Act, 20 U. S. C.§ 1400 P.L., 108–446 (2004).

Johnson, Evelyn S. (2014). Understanding why a child is struggling to learn: The role of cognitive processing evaluation in learning disability identification. *Topics in Language Disorders, 34*, 59–73.

Mellard, D. F., & Johnson, E. (2008). *RTI: A practitioners guide to implementing response to intervention.* Corwin Press.

Nelson, J. R., Benner G. J., & Mooney, P. (2013). *Instructional practices for students with behavioral disorders: Strategies for reading, writing, and math.* Guildford Press.

No Child Left Behind Act of 2001, 20 U. S. C. 70 § 6301 *et seq.*

Substance Abuse and Mental Health Services Administration. (2020). *SAMHSA's annual mental health, substance use data provide roadmap for future action.* Retrieved June 18, 2023. https://www.samhsa.gov/newsroom/press-announcements /202009110221.

Walker, H. M., Horner, R. H., Sugai, G., Bullis, M., Sprague, J. R., Bricker, D., & Kaufman, M. J. (1996). Integrated approaches to preventing anti-social behavior patterns among school-aged children and youth. *Journal of Emotional and Behavioral Disorders 4,* 194–209.

Williams, D. D. (2015). *An RTI guide to improving the performance of African American children.* Thousand Oaks, CA: Corwin Publishing.

World Health Organization. (2023). Adolescent and young adult health. Retrieved May 10, 2023. https://www.who.int/news-room/fact-sheets/detail/adolescents -health-risks-and-solutions.

Chapter 2

Equity and Belonging Achieved Through Community Engagement, Involvement, and Sustainability in Schools

OUTCOMES DON'T LIE: CURRENT EDUCATION SYSTEMS ARE NOT ACHIEVING EQUITABLE OUTCOMES

The population of students in public schools has become increasingly diverse, and behavior management outcomes and practices vary greatly among cultural groups (Fallon et al., 2012). Yet, the current mode of operation in schools in the United States maintains racial power and further marginalizes communities that are non-dominant (Bal, 2016). When we talk about MTSS, the need for a definition that is operational for diverse culture is important because of the changing demographics in schools and concerns about problem behavior, most importantly in the context of negative outcomes for culturally and linguistically diverse students (Sugai et al., 2012).

Obtaining the highest positive outcomes for all students when implementing MTSS warrants leaders to ensure it is culturally responsive and centers belonging. Past research has shown that while office referrals and suspensions decrease and academics improve, discrepancies in outcomes among groups of students still exist (Heidelburg & Collins, 2023). Even with these mixed results, MTSS displays evidence of the positive student outcomes that so many schools are seeking (Scott et al., 2019). Thus, there is an opportunity for leaders to look deep into their MTSS work and to improve their outcomes for all students. Accomplishing this starts with creating a culture of belonging for all. This work must come from the heart and must be the foundation of our collective, culturally responsive implementation of MTSS.

Cobb and Krownapple (2019) define belonging as experiencing appreciation, validation, acceptance, and fair treatment within an environment. The work of implementation should center on understanding and building relationships with the folx in your communities to sustain and cultivate belonging within MTSS. No one solution exists that will transform schools to impact disparities in educational opportunities and outcomes (Bal et al., 2016). Coupled with belonging, a school's approach to discipline must be associated with the behavior and not the student (McNeill et al., 2016). These approaches must be thoughtful, evidence-based, and centered in belonging to avoid further harm to all learners, especially the most marginalized students.

It is essential to reimagine the implementation of MTSS to center on community and belonging. This results in children being viewed as active participants in their environments and ensures that the impact of a child's environment on their behavior is considered (Heidelburg et al., 2022). Academic and behavioral interventions and their implementation require great effort and should not be done in isolation from one another. Practitioners have tried to combine evidence-based approaches but have still fallen short in both implementation and reduction of racial disparities in disciplinary outcomes (Heidelburg et al., 2022) Sometimes bold and uncomfortable steps need to be taken toward cultural change (Loper et al., 2021), and the use of adaptation, belonging, and equity can help us all keep moving in the best direction for all learners.

WHAT CAN LEADERS DO?

An employee cannot change their cultural or linguistic background. Nevertheless, steps can be taken to help them to further understand the backgrounds of the learners they serve. Leaders can build processes that encourage school staff to reflect on how they show up and the relationships they build with students, families, and members of the local community. As Brene Brown (2017) reminds us, "True belonging doesn't require us to change who we are. It requires us to be who we are." Critical race pedagogy notes race informs the culture of schools (Ledesma & Calderón, 2015), and school staff are encouraged to use cultural referents in pedagogy (Ladson-Billings, 1995). It is important for staff to increase their knowledge of parents' and students' distinctive cultures and characteristics (Kourea et al., 2016). Defining culture and context for schools is crucial to begin to understand staff, students, and parents and to create more inclusive discipline practices. Defining culture has been difficult and done differently depending on the legal, political, and educational perspectives of those involved (Sugai et al., 2012).

Multiple research studies have attempted to tackle defining culture in their work (Fallon et al., 2012; Sugai et al., 2012; Vincent et al., 2011). This work has stemmed from the need to understand the various backgrounds of students in schools so MTSS systems can be built to support them. Leaders should approach MTSS considering the four central components of connectedness, inclusivity, equity, and relevant learning opportunities. These provide a platform to create positive changes. Because influencing the social and academic success of students is related to cultural factors (Fallon et al., 2012), these factors must be taken into consideration. From Knoster's (2018) viewpoint, culturally competent approaches are needed and must be emphasized in endeavors to reach diverse students. Thus, practically defining culture can limit cultural misunderstanding (Sugai et al., 2012).

Natesan et al. (2011) noted that understanding the instructional and educational needs of African-American students is a challenge for teachers. Within MTSS, schools can develop structures of support and strategies that are built to address the diverse needs of students so greater outcomes can be achieved for all students, regardless of their cultural backgrounds (Vincent et al., 2011). Understanding culture and context can be a crucial lever in changing both a school's climate and a school's MTSS implementation. The key to this understanding is to focus on connectedness to build relationships with students and their families.

This strategic focus on building relationships can assist in improving a classroom's environment and ultimately a school's MTSS implementation (Howard et al., 2020). Educators have an opportunity to see the cultural distinctions in diverse family dynamics (Kourea et al., 2016) by viewing behaviors from a cultural and contextual lens (Sugai et al., 2012). This understanding can inform behavioral decisions, even minor occurrences, and give more attention to the academic efforts necessary for continued achievement. It should be noted that implementation can be improved by considering the context, learning history, and culture of families, students, community members, and staff (Sugai et al., 2012). Building and refining MTSS must take into consideration the cultural and linguistic dynamics of all stakeholders. It is essential to figure out when the pain of cultural misunderstanding is felt in the implementation process, so trust is increased in communities. H.E.L.P. (see figure 2.1) is on the way.

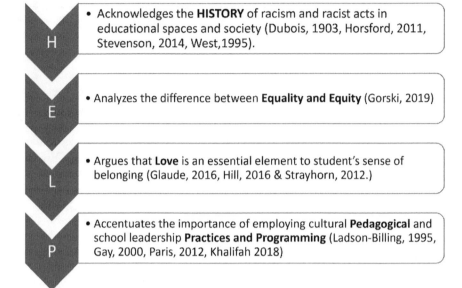

Figure 2.1.   The H.E.L.P. Framework, Whitaker (2021).

THE MTSS TEAM AND COMMUNITY ENGAGEMENT

The journey of building an equitable mindset to cultivate belonging within MTSS must start with what it really takes to sustain this particular environment. Dewey (1916) defined the environment as "conditions that promote or hinder activities of a living being" (p. 14). As much as educators enjoy seeing the positive results from data and evidence-based practices, they rarely discuss the process to get there. Each person comes to the work with something. This is where the work of the MTSS team really begins. It truly starts with you. Remember a tool is only as good as its user. Recalling the definition of MTSS, "the overarching referent for frameworks designed to target academic and behavioral challenges with a focus on a tiered continuum of evidence-based practices within the context of prevention science and implementation research" (Freeman et al., 2017), educators should start to look at the user and recipient of the framework. Recipients of this framework are inclusive of the learners and the communities in which they dwell.

Who knows the learners? Everyone in the community in which a learner lives, and the goal of that community is everyone thriving. The teachers, staff, parents, administrators, the local grocer, salon owners, and even barbers are all a part of the implementation process, and thus all should thrive. The planning of MTSS in schools must leverage the bonds the community has with a school and the community's involvement in the implementation of the framework. First, it is necessary to define community and the intersection of MTSS, belonging, and equity. The foundational definition of a community is derived from a key community member, who happened to be a barber. The most impactful resource any community has is human capital—that is, engaged citizens. The Kettering Foundation noted how relationships shifted when citizens focused on a shared vision for youth and their community (Harbour, 2015). Citizens of different races, economic and cultural backgrounds, beliefs, and political persuasion worked together to achieve mutual goals (Harbour, 2015). In our work, we should collaborate with these "engaged citizens" that already are in service to our learners.

VIGNETTE FROM A CONVERSATION WITH A NEIGHBORHOOD BARBER ILLUSTRATING COMMUNITY

A barber from Paterson, New Jersey made a wonderful point about community, which can be useful to the planning and implementation of MTSS (McDowell & Levitas, 1994):

> It's been a business throughout the ages; everybody likes to get dressed up and to get dressed up without a haircut is not completely dressed up. The barber's duty, his line in the life of a neighborhood, is to keep people groomed, keep people looking well, keep people—sometimes even the barber has been a place where men could come and pour out their troubles to. Sometimes they have gotten, had, an argument or disagreement with their wives, and an experienced barber could say, "Oh no, it shouldn't be like that." While you're working with someone, working on a person's face, his body, you can get a little closer to him. In other words, you're right by his ear anyway and he's got to hear you anyway. So, this way, you're a little closer to him and you have the advantage to talk to him. Some barbers have been in the neighborhood for years. I cut your grandfather's hair. I cut your father's hair. Now, I'm cutting your hair, and then I'll be cutting your kids' hair. This has happened to me. When I first opened up here, the kids that were ten years old are forty-something years old and have grandchildren. It's a very important place in a neighborhood, like years ago: first the home, the church, and the school. Then when it comes down to the neighborhood: the grocery store, the barber, the butcher. They all fall in line making up the community.

The community has a responsibility to support what is happening in our environments, and educators can leverage this power by remembering community in our practice. Differences must not only be tolerated but seen as necessary polarities between which creative dialogue can spark. Only then does the necessity for interdependency become nonthreatening. Only within that interdependency of these different strengths, acknowledged and equal, can the power to seek new ways of being in the world generate, as well as the courage and sustenance to act where there are no charters (Lorde, 2007). The tools and strategies in MTSS can be used to center community and build a framework in which difference of thought and lived experience is seen as a strength.

CREATING AN MTSS THAT IS COMMUNITY-CENTERED AND CULTURALLY RESPONSIVE

Creating an MTSS that is both community-centered and culturally responsive is not an easy undertaking, but there are intentional steps leaders can take when they begin or revise their MTSS framework. The leader in a building or district must understand the need to recruit and keep culturally responsive teachers and staff who are better prepared to work with students of color (Khalifa et al., 2016). Continuing to work with culturally responsive staff to enhance these school-wide measures will ensure more equitable practices in outcomes. Thus, MTSS implementation plans should be reviewed with the entire school team periodically to ensure the student population is reflected in its practice.

The efforts of the school-based team are instrumental for MTSS to ultimately be successful. Yet this success must be sustained by supportive policy and systematic efforts on the district level of a school system. Investing in development of effective leaders becomes a critical part of the process of retaining and recruiting the best staff for students who have been marginalized (Khalifa et al., 2016). Bal et al. (2016) also emphasized the need for school districts to examine disciplinary practices and to transform the current system that produces racial disparities. Districts can shift funding priorities to provide coaching support to school staff with the implementation of MTSS. With the massive fiscal cuts and hiring rates in education, MTSS can reduce the need for behavioral 1:1 interventions, and those funds can be reallocated to supports aligned with greatest need.

While trying to recruit and increase staff, a focus on improving efforts to diversify the teaching population in communities is crucial. As the student population in schools has become more diverse, the teaching field remains mostly White and female (Natesan et al., 2011; Will, 2020). This data is reflected in the national population of the teaching field, which may not reflect the population in your environment. This focus on hiring and diversifying your staff will "build collective muscle for equitable implementation"

(Loper et al., 2021). A focus on training and support for culturally responsive approaches is also necessary for the continual improvement of classroom, disciplinary, and teaching practices. Districts and schools need to give sufficient time to professional development with regard to culturally responsive approaches and classroom management (Skiba & Losen, 2015). Culturally relevant pedagogy in coaching and training can assist teachers in responding to behavior from students whose backgrounds may not mirror their own. Districts must provide staff with examples of culturally relevant teaching in both theory and practice (Ladson-Billings, 1995). Active engagement with urban communities and schools will open conversations with educators and students of color (Hines-Datiri, 2015). It is essential for this work to be long-term, and to include engaging in dialogue that mandates teachers to be aware of the needs of minority students (Whitford et al., 2016).

An example of a culturally responsive strategy seen in some communities is starting the day with a song, before proceeding with the rest of the day. Others may use affirmations or pledges during this time. This practice is usually used to set intentions for the day. In some environments, they chant affirmations as a school community at the end of the day. Even parents know these chants and cheers! This is a small act in dismantling a system of oppression that says we all cannot start every day and end it with intention and clarity. Where in your MTSS can you adapt to bring this sense of belonging to your environment?

Exclusionary policies and the subsequent discipline disparities they create for racialized groups are reflective of the constant influence race has on United States society. Discipline disparities by race and the strong differences in the life experiences of racial groups are likely an implicit consequence of a long history of biases and stereotypes that influence policy and procedures in the United States (Carter et al., 2017). These disparities and divisions manifest in many systems, including prisons and schools. Swain and Noblit (2011) stated that education systems operate as punitive societies. In their research, they explored where the educational and the prison systems intersect, by examining zero-tolerance policies in schools to explore the history of race and segregation. They also evaluated the persecution of minorities under federally guided practices and focused on the power structures used to segregate people of color, noting that a school's disciplinary exclusion process is a vehicle aligned to create avenues for criminal activity. Finally, the authors concluded that disproportionality in discipline is a rising concern. The school-to-prison pipeline is very real. If this is not recognized and addressed, the implementation of MTSS and any other framework can and will be oppressive.

Chapter 2

MAKE IT BETTER BY FACING IT TOGETHER

"If you have come here to help me, you are wasting your time. But if you have come because your liberation is bound up with mine, then let us work together."

—*Lilla Watson (and Community)*

This quote is attributed to Lilla Watson, although a community of folx, specifically the Aboriginal Activists in Queensland, co-constructed this statement. Applied to the context of MTSS, it means that we need to use our roles in schools as tools of liberation. In the article "Ethics from the Margins," they share that poet bell hooks claims to have found solace, comfort, and liberation through the written word. They note that she began to develop her keen sense and theory of justice and privilege as a young girl watching both her father and her brother enjoy a disproportionate authority and control in family and community matters as well as learning from her grandfather's more just ways.

Because our liberation is bound up with each other, we must bind together to curate more culturally responsive MTSS. This can be done in more than just one way. It must be centered on belonging so all folx you are in service to feel validated and appreciated. As implementers, we are bound together in this MTSS work. Imagine what happens when we can truly collaborate as an educational community during conferences, professional development, or even in our daily environment. It is hard to collaborate with folx. It may be a painful process to do the work of looking at data and bringing people into the larger school community to help us give every learner what they need to be successful.

But, with the right care and attention to communication, folx will come in because they can feel our work with learners is tied up with them. Community becomes like family who may lack skills in collaboration but can gain them as we do the work together. We have to hold a collective belief that when you win, we all win. How many of us are creating seats for folx as part of our leadership moves? Let's start demonstrating what a true community should look like with the MTSS framework. The work is always unfinished but who you surround yourself with in your work is invaluable. The great and late Nipsey Hussle says, if you look around the room, and you don't get inspired, you are not in a circle, you're in a cage. Reflect on the folx in your circle, and who needs to be there to do your work. Build a team so strong that one of your team members would remind a colleague they can take a day off. Create teams where someone brings you a cup of coffee because a meeting is about to start. The MTSS team should be a safe, welcoming circle of committed community members of your environment.

"Pedagogy, regardless of its name, is useless without teachers dedicated to challenging systemic oppression with intersectional social justice"

— *Dr. Bettina Love*

There is something that you, as the practitioner/leader, can do to prepare for the work of creating MTSS in your environment that reflects your community. List all the things *you* have to do in a week. Separate them into categories. Go for it! You lead the charge on what "data" we should look at. I would highly suggest, at a minimum, adding these: Work, Home, and Fun. What makes you tick? What is your structure of joy? This is your framework. If you are human, there are times that you must adapt this framework to get maximum use from this thing called life. This same concept could assist in implementing MTSS, with equity, belonging, and community at the center. We agree with our colleagues McIntosh and Goodman (2016) and Gettinger and Stoiber (2016) about systems and structures: One of the most powerful parts of the implementation of MTSS is the actual framework built and sustained in a variety of educational spaces.

A PERSONAL STATEMENT FROM
AUTHOR ERIKA MCDOWELL

We must be committed to using data and understanding the history of our work as practitioners. We need to shift our implementation from a *you* approach to a *with* mindset. We must get good at seeing people for who they are. It first starts with making authentic and rich relationships to connect with the community you are in service to. Which side are you going to be on? Are you going to tell people that it's in your environment? We need to change. It's been a long time since I ever wore my hair in faux locs. I used to have it pressed. You'll see a picture. I did it because I felt I had to lean into dominant culture. Don't use code-switching. I don't have to lean into dominant culture because there's nothing wrong with the culture that I'm from. Are you asking people, "You know what community of resistance—What are we going to do to change, so everybody feels good here?" We have a responsibility. You've got to talk to people. We've got to get clear on how people doing in your environment.

We got to get in dialogue with our parents. How many people talk to folks' parents? I appreciated people walking up to Mary and Warren McDowell and saying, "Can you tell me a little more about Erika?" My mother always says to me: "I never wanted to kill your spirit." How would you know about me if you didn't ask my mother about this spirit that I have? So, we've got to get talking to folks. Instead of implementers stating, "I'm going to do equity, I'm going to do diversity, I'm going to . . . "—go work on community. Work on it, because we all know what it feels like to belong and to not belong. You've got enough tools to cultivate community and belonging.

TOOLS TO H.E.L.P

Lack of belonging and equitable practices for all is an emergent concern, and addressing this issue must be tackled at all levels in our education system. The history of race in America must be reviewed and discussed to trace how racial disproportionality has grown. Also, the history of education and the major decisions that were made to equalize the school experience for all students must be reflected upon for its effectiveness. "For MTSS to be fully realized . . . racial discrimination, poverty, denials of constitutional liberties, or inequalities in educational opportunities must not be tolerated" (Francis-Thompson, 2017). Disproportionality issues in schools are in need of an adaptable, equitable framework that considers the cultural and contextual shifts in schools today. Dr. Ronald Whitaker's H.E.L.P. framework (figure 2.1) can be a tool used in conjunction with MTSS to ensure every learner is safe and whole in the work.

Great has been your faithfulness to the work, yet we have more to do. More work for you, for our environments, and most of all our learners and their communities. Everyone reading this book may not have the biggest budget, structures, and systems. But what do you have? *You.* You are the greatest and dearest tool we have in dismantling systems of oppression. This oppression impacts us too and we must walk into a season of implementation that centers on our most beloved. These strategies can impact your implementation to be responsive and inclusive. Look at how you have done so far. Very similar to when children were in summer camp and ended each day with a chant: *We shall conclude this chapter with an affirmation and chant:*

> MTSS can and will . . .
> Center Equity Through Community Engagement, Involvement, and Sustainability,
> Lean into a Pedagogy of love and belonging,
> With H.E.L.P and Liberation,
> And because you have this book,
> My Environment,
> Our Learners,
> With Community,

We can leverage the greatest tools in our collective toolboxes
responsibly!
Let's get to the adaptive, liberating, and transformational MTSS
work ahead!
Remember community! You need someone to come into your circle
to randomly just say,
YOU GOT THIS!

REFERENCES

Bal, A., Schrader, E. M., Afacan, K., & Mawene, D. (2016). Using learning labs for culturally responsive positive behavioral interventions and supports. *Intervention in School and Clinic, 52*(2), 122–128.

Brown, B. (2017). *Braving the wilderness: The quest for true belonging and the courage to stand alone* (First ed.). Random House.

Carter, P. L., Skiba, R., Arredondo, M. I., & Pollock, M. (2017). You can't fix what you don't look at: Acknowledging race in addressing racial discipline disparities. *Urban Education, 52*(2), 207–235.

Cobb, F., & Krownapple, J. (2019). *Belonging through a culture of dignity: The keys to successful equity implementation.* Mimi & Todd Press.

Dewey, J. (1916). *Democracy and education: An introduction to the philosophy of education.* New York: Macmillan.

Fallon, L. M., O'Keeffe, B. V., & Sugai, G. (2012). Consideration of culture and context in school-wide positive behavior support: A review of current literature. *Journal of Positive Behavior Interventions, 14*(4), 209–219. doi: 10.1177/1098300712442242.

Francis-Thompson, N. (2017). *Beyond the pink sand: Case studies of experiences of multi-tier system of supports implementation in the Bermuda Public School system.* ProQuest Dissertations Publishing.

Freeman, J., Sugai, G., Simonsen, B., & Everett, S. (2017). MTSS coaching: Bridging knowing to doing. *Theory into Practice, 56*(1), 29–37.

Gettinger, M., & Stoiber, K. C. (2016). Coaching and demonstration of evidence-based book-reading practices: Effects on Head Start teachers' literacy-related behaviors and classroom environment. *Journal of Early Childhood Teacher Education, 37*(2), 117–141.

Harbour, P. M. (2015). Communities—A Resource: Broadening the definition of education. *National Civic Review, 104*(1).

Heidelburg, K., & Collins, T. A. (2023). Development of *Black to Success*: A culturally enriched social skills program for Black adolescent males. *School Psychology Review, 52*(3), 316–329.

Heidelburg, K., Rutherford, L., & Parks, T. W. (2022). A preliminary analysis assessing SWPBIS implementation fidelity in relation to disciplinary outcomes of Black students in urban schools. *Urban Review, 54*, 138–154.

Hines-Datiri, D. (2015). When police intervene: Race, gender, and discipline of Black male students at an urban high school. *Journal of Cases in Educational Leadership, 18*(2), 122–133.

Howard, J. R., Milner-McCall, T., Howard, T. C., Cruz, M. C., & Duke, N. K. (2020, March 13). *No more teaching without positive relationships*. Heinemann Publishing.

Khalifa, M. A., Gooden, M. A., & Davis, J. E. (2016). Culturally responsive school leadership: A synthesis of the literature. *Review of Educational Research, 86*, 1272–1311. doi: 10.3102/0034654316630383.

Knoster, T. (2018). Commentary: Evolution of positive behavior support and future directions. *Journal of Positive Behavior Interventions, 20*(1), 23–26. doi: 10.1177/1098300717735056.

Kourea, L., Lo, Y., & Owens, T. L. (2016). Using parental input from Black families to increase cultural responsiveness for teaching SWPBS expectations. *Behavioral Disorders, 41*, 226–240.

Ladson-Billings, G. (1995). Toward a theory of culturally relevant pedagogy. *American Educational Research Journal, 32*, 465–491. doi: 10.2307/1163320.

Ledesma, M. C., & Calderón, D. (2015). Critical race theory in education: A review of past literature and a look to the future. *Qualitative Inquiry, 21*(3), 206–222.

Loper, A., Woo, B., & Metz, A. (2021). Equity is fundamental to implementation science. *Stanford Social Innovation Review, 19*(3), A3–A5.

Lorde, A. (2007). The transformation of silence into language and action. In *Sister outsider: Essays and speeches* (pp. 40–44). New York: Crossing Press.

McCallum, Tom. (2019). Do the People in Your Circle Inspire You? https://tommccallum.com/2019/05/03/do-the-people-in-your-circle-inspire-you/.

McDowell, R. L., & Levitas, S. (1994). *Sometimes even the barber has been a place where men could come and pour out their troubles to.* 1994-08-30. [Audio] Retrieved from the Library of Congress. www.loc.gov/item/afcwip002842.

McIntosh, K., & Goodman, S. (2016). *Integrated multi-tiered systems of support: Blending RTI and PBIS.* Guilford Press.

McNeill, K. F., Friedman, B. D., & Chavez, C. (2016). Keep them so you can teach them: Alternatives to exclusionary discipline. *International Public Health Journal, 8*(2), 169.

Mellard, D. F., & Johnson, E. S. (2008). Response to intervention: A practitioner's guide to implementation. Corwin Press.

Monroe, C. R. (2005). Why are "bad boys" always Black? Causes of disproportionality in school discipline and recommendations for change. *The Clearing House: A Journal of Educational Strategies, Issues and Ideas, 79*(1), 45–50.

Natesan, P., Webb-Hasan, G. C., Carter, N. P., & Walter, P. (2011). Validity of the cultural awareness and beliefs inventory of urban teachers: A parallel mixed methods study. *International Journal of Multiple Research Approaches, 5*(2), 238–253.

Scott, T. M., Gage, N. A., Hirn, R. G., Lingo, A. S., & Burt, J. (2019). An examination of the association between MTSS implementation fidelity measures and student outcomes. *Preventing School Failure, 63*(4), 308–316.

Skiba, R. J., & Losen, D. J. (2015). From reaction to prevention: Turning the page on school discipline. *American Educator, 39*(4), 4.

Souto☐Manning, M., Martinez, D. C., & Musser, A. D. (2022). ELA as English language abolition: Toward a pedagogy of communicative belonging. *Reading Research Quarterly, 57*(4), 1089–1106.

Sugai, G., O'Keeffe, B. V., & Fallon, L. M. (2012). A contextual consideration of culture and school-wide positive behavior support. *Journal of Positive Behavior Interventions, 14*(4), 197–208.

Swain, A. E., & Noblit, G. W. (2011). Education in a punitive society: An introduction. *The Urban Review, 43*(4), 465–475. doi: 10.1007/s11256-011-0186-x.

Valdivia, A. N. (2002). bell hooks: Ethics from the margins. *Qualitative Inquiry, 8*(4), 429–447.

Vincent, C. G., Randall, C., Cartledge, G., Tobin, T. J., & Swain-Bradway, J. (2011). Toward a conceptual integration of cultural responsiveness and schoolwide positive behavior support. *Journal of Positive Behavior Interventions, 13*, 219–229. doi: 10.1177/1098300711399765.

Whitaker, R. (2021). *Assistant Dean of education introduces framework to create racial equity in schools.* Introduces HELP Framework for Education Equity. https://www.cabrini.edu/about/media-hub/news/2021/ronald-whitaker-introduces-help-framework-for-education-equity.

Whitford, D. K., Katsiyannis, A., & Counts, J. (2016). Discriminatory discipline: Trends and issues. *NASSP Bulletin, 100*(2), 117–135.

Will, M. (2020, April 14). Still mostly White and female: New federal data on the teaching profession. *Education Week.*

Wright, J., Whitaker, R. W., Khalifa, M., & Briscoe, F. (2020). The color of neoliberal reform: A critical race policy analysis of school district takeovers in Michigan. *Urban Education* (Beverly Hills, Calif.), *55*(3), 424–447.

Chapter 3

Using Implementation Science to Support the Integration Process

THE ROLE OF IMPLEMENTATION SCIENCE IN MTSS

Once a district has clearly defined their purpose and the goals to achieve desired outcomes, the use of implementation science can serve as both an entry point and a roadmap for systematic implementation. Implementation Science (Fixsen et al., 2009) uses four stages of implementation that assist systems and organizations to successfully adopt a new initiative or practice and align it with other existing initiatives or practices. Implementation science can be applied to any organizational initiative. The focus here is on the research completed and practices used during the past two decades that involve the use of implementation science to support implementation of MTSS.

Applying the stages of implementation science described in table 3.1 to the framework of MTSS is not a linear process. The implementation of any major initiative is an iterative process and involves continuous analysis of both process and outcomes (Fixsen et al., 2009). Implementation science has shown us that evidence-informed practices, initiatives, programs, frameworks, strategies, and tools can be developed, but will continue to have disparate outcomes until applying them with fidelity in practice improves. The four implementation stages are summarized in the following table.

Implementation science can build a bridge from research to practice. An important resource for district and school teams is the Implementation Stages Planning Tool that can be found on the State Implementation and Scaling-up of Evidenced-based Practices (SISEP, 2023) website which is part of the National Implementation Research Network (NIRN, 2023).

School systems are always responding to the ongoing changes in policies and priorities. Without this integration, initiatives compete against

Table 3.1: Stages of Implementation

Implementation Stages	Key Questions to Ask:
Exploration—Identify the need for change, compare possible approaches to achieve change. and assess readiness for change.	Do we have all interested parties' voices at the table when we explore this approach? Will an MTSS approach help us to reach our outcome goals? What are the measurable goals we hope to accomplish? Are we ready to begin MTSS?
Installation—Identify the needed supports to put the practice in place with good fidelity. Gather feedback from those who will be affected.	Do we have all interested parties voice at the table when we install this approach? Have we invested in initial training needed for implementation?
Initial Implementation—Expand training, coaching and data review to support the new skills and practices, and improvement in implementation.	Do we have all interested parties voice at the table when we implement this approach?
Full Implementation—The innovation is well-integrated into the daily practice and routines. It remains in place through administrative changes.	How are we using the voice of all interested parties voice to continually innovate our process for implementation?

one another or have fragmented approaches that cannot be sustained. Metz et al. (2020) from NIRN state, "we can continue to research and develop evidence-informed practices, programs and policies, and implementation theories, frameworks, strategies and tools, but until we get better at applying them in practice, outcomes will not improve." Implementation science helps provide us with the needed tools to apply the practices and to make progress.

When making the decision to implement MTSS, school and district leaders should consider the contextual conditions for implementation. Metz, Woo, and Loper (2021) identify three contextual conditions that district and leadership teams must consider: macro, organizational, and local. The macro context refers to the larger socio-political and economic factors that may either promote or impede implementation. For example, when there is pressure to increase staff salaries in a district, spending on a new initiative may not be supported. The organizational context refers to the existing culture and climate within a district or school that may affect how individuals and teams behave. This is often phrased as, "But this is how we have always done it! Why change?" The local context refers to other school or community activities and relationships that may positively or negatively impact implementation. If a school or district is already undertaking several other major initiatives, it may be harder to implement MTSS with high fidelity.

A school or district may benefit from either hiring an MTSS implementation support specialist directly or contracting with an outside organization to support implementation. These specialists can help a district to go through the initial exploration and readiness process and then to apply and integrate the implementation strategies and approaches found within the stages of implementation. There are excellent resources to assist implementation support specialists located on the NIRN website mentioned previously.

It is critical to high quality implementation to assure that all needed voices and perspectives are heard and that they are incorporated into decisions about implementation. Bal et al. (2016) described equitable implementation occurring "when strong equity components (including explicit attention to the culture, history, values, and needs of the community) are integrated into the principles and tools of implementation science to facilitate quality implementation of effective programs for a specific community or group of communities."

STRATEGIES AND RESOURCES FOR
THE EXPLORATION STAGE

A common misstep for districts and schools is to move directly to training staff to use a new program, practice, or initiative that they think will be a solution to a need that has risen. Instead, the exploration stage encourages schools to pause and spend time reviewing the program, practice, or initiative against other possible solutions to ensure it is the best fit. It also directs the schools or district to spend time gathering the opinions of all stakeholders to make sure the needed buy-in is present.

Research has indicated that educators can struggle to transfer evidence-based practices into the school setting with high fidelity (Powell et al., 2015). In the exploration stage, schools and districts examine the environment and activities needed to successfully install a new practice with consistency. What will the training content include? What opportunities exist for coaching implementation? Are there existing policies or practices that should be put on hold or eliminated to create bandwidth for new strategies?

Eber et al. (2019) remind us that "regardless of the motivation for change, it is essential that organizations invest in an exploration process to ensure (a) the proposed new approach or initiative is a good fit with identified needs, and (b) that the structures are in place to support implementation efforts that will produce a measurable impact."

To lead this exploratory stage, schools and districts should assemble an implementation team that is representative of the district staff and larger community (parents, students, and community members). This team will oversee and guide the implementation of MTSS. It is important that this team have the needed knowledge, skills, and authority to oversee the work and make any needed policy and practice changes. If such a team already exists within the school or district and they have the capacity to lead this process, then they may take on the work.

To ensure equity of perspectives, it is important to include the voices of those who may be or have been traditionally marginalized in your community. Schools typically have several different committees to address various needs in their buildings. Prior to developing a new committee to address or oversee MTSS implementation at any tier, it is essential to consider all existing teams. The purpose of this review is to investigate whether there is any significant overlap in committee function or purpose and/or to identify teams or initiatives that may no longer be useful.

CORE ELEMENTS OF A PRODUCTIVE COMMITTEE

In education, staff are often brought together to address a need but without the conditions needed for productive teamwork and effective decision-making. To be effective, a district or school team/committee should contain several core elements. Prior to holding meetings, committees should first identify key features related to successful interaction as a team. First and foremost, all committees should have a clear purpose and mission to clarify the priorities and activities with which the committee is tasked. Additionally, a committee should assign roles to all team members. Core roles can include:

- facilitator
- minute-taker
- timekeeper
- data analyst
- active participants

When each committee member has a clearly delineated role and function, meetings can be more effective and efficient. Committees should also establish group norms for interaction and should clarify agreements about expected behaviors. All committees should predetermine a yearly meeting schedule to ensure attendance of at least 80% of team members at all meetings. Finally, establishing a communication plan that indicates a target audience, communication mechanism, and responsible party is helpful in streamlining committee functions and ensuring information is provided to all necessary parties in a timely manner.

Teams should continually evaluate their meetings to determine if they are running effectively and meeting foundations are in place. Some examples of meeting foundations include:

- starting and ending meetings on time
- using a shared agenda
- having clearly defined committee roles
- engaging in productive problem solving
- determining and delineating a course of action to address identified problems
- completing tasks as assigned

Research on a model for problem solving in team meetings called Team Initiated Problem Solving (TIPS) indicates that using these core meeting foundations increases efficiency, leads to better outcomes, and saves time and money (Horner et al., 2018; Todd et al., 2011).

HOW DOES YOUR TEAM BEGIN THIS WORK?

Following the Implementation Stages Planning Tool, the leadership team may want to start with a root cause analysis to clearly define the needs that MTSS will address, and then assess what is currently in place to support the rollout of the initiative. A needs assessment tool can also help a school or district explore the need for MTSS. A needs and reediness assessment that can be used for exploring MTSS in elementary and secondary settings is available on the Massachusetts Department of Education website at https://matoolsforschools.com.

Metz and Louison's (2018) hexagon tool (figure 3.1) is also helpful. This NIRN tool can be used in the exploration stage to assess if an initiative or program will truly meet the identified needs. It can be used later in implementation as a tool to help increase fit and feasibility. The tool uses six contextual fit and feasibility indicators: need, evidence, fit, usability, capacity, and supports. A visual is provided in figure 3.1, but to use the tool, download it and the instruction book available for free on the NIRN website.

STRATEGIES AND RESOURCES FOR
THE INSTALLATION STAGES

Once a school or district has completed the exploration process, the next step is to identify the needed supports to put practices in place with good

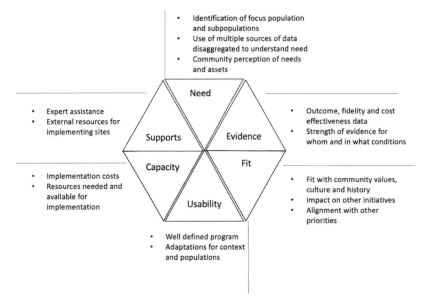

Figure 3.1.   Hexagon Tool

fidelity. A key step here is to develop a transparent process to gather feedback from *all* interested stakeholders who may be affected by MTSS. This includes leadership, staff, students, families, and community members. In education, we have all experienced initiative fatigue, so it is important to ensure that implementation of MTSS is not just seen as "one more thing" added to already full plates or as another top-down change being forced on schools.

It is essential for all persons affected by MTSS to understand what MTSS is and the benefits it will bring to your school or district. Professional development at this stage should be about developing a shared understanding of MTSS, gaining buy-in of all stakeholders, and building the capacity to support implementation. Districts and schools may want to conduct an initiatives inventory to assess what current programs and supports are already in place (see chapter 8). If a district or school is focusing on a certain outcome of MTSS, such as behavior or reading, then they may want to look more specifically at those programs and supports.

A key aspect of the installation phase is to develop a clearly articulated vision and implementation plan for the work to be accomplished. The implementation plan should outline the measurable goals to be accomplished through the implementation of MTSS. If implemented at the district level, district leadership should determine whether it will be more effective to implement a cohort model where a certain number of schools are brought on board each year, or if all schools will move toward implementation at once.

Often the size of a district, the budget, staff capacity and the current implementation of other initiatives are considerations.

Once the components to support the implementation are in place, the district or school is ready to train all staff in MTSS. Assuming that all invested parties have been provided training to develop a basic understanding of MTSS, the focus now shifts to more in-depth training for those staff who are directly leading and implementing the work. A great example of this is when a school or district is focused on MTSS for behavior, which has various training needs for all staff depending upon their role. It is recommended that at least a core group of key staff receive training before beginning initial implementation.

STRATEGIES AND RESOURCES FOR INITIAL IMPLEMENTATION

As a school or district heads into initial implementation they will need to expand upon the inaugural training done in the installation phase and invest in coaching as they move forward with implementation. The use of coaching has been shown critical to successful implementation of key practices and strategies (Kraft et al., 2018). MTSS coaches can provide skill development and guidance in real time. There are several tools found on the NIRN and National Technical Assistance Center for PBIS websites to assist with coaching. A coaching services delivery plan (see chapter 8) can help a school or district to best use the coaching supports.

During the implementation stage, the district or school leadership team should convene at least monthly and review both fidelity of practice and outcomes data to support the ongoing improvement of implementation. To monitor progress, the data that a team uses should come from multiple sources, including staff, students, families, and other interested parties. Having a mixture of hard data and perceptions or "street data" (Safir & Dugan, 2021) can help provide the best picture of the impacts of implementation.

If not using one already, the team should adopt a process to use the data for decision-making and to refine the implementation infrastructure (i.e., training, coaching, data systems, leadership supports and resources). One example of a data process is the Team Initiated Problem Solving (TIPS) process mentioned earlier in this chapter, which adds needed structure to a team for increased efficiency and effectiveness and in using uses data for decision-making. More on the TIPS process can be found on the pbis.org website by searching for TIPS.

During this phase, ongoing professional development will help schools and districts to continue to grow and develop their MTSS implementation.

While some districts may have the staff and expertise to provide this training on their own, others may need to seek training support from outside agencies. We encourage schools and districts to use trainers who align themselves with national work supported by the Department of Education and the National PBIS Technical Assistance Center. Training needs should be driven by data that is being collected at this stage.

STRATEGIES AND RESOURCES FOR
FULL IMPLEMENTATION

A school or district will likely find that they reach full implementation in stages that are often related to specific tiers. Schools and districts often focus first on tier 1 or universal components before working on tiers 2 and 3. Some schools and districts focus on implementation across tiers all at once. A model for this type of implementation can be found at the Ci3T website (https://www.ci3t.org/about). Once full implementation is met, it is important to remember that the work is not complete. Rather, a school or district moves into a phase of sustainability and continuous renewal.

At this point, MTSS should be ingrained in the culture of the district or school and become something that everyone consistently implements. For continued sustainability, it is important that the leadership team continues to meet regularly and that the review of data cycles remains strong. As staff turnover occurs, there must be a systematic process to train new staff to the MTSS process. Many schools and districts have general training on MTSS for all staff as well as role-specific training.

Teams will want to maintain the use of continual feedback loops to communicate about progress and next steps. The leadership team should also ensure that any new policies and procedures or changes to existing policies and procedures support the implementation of MTSS. District and school communication and policy, both internal and external, should include details on MTSS implementation. Many districts aid sustainability by creating an MTSS facilitator position at the district level.

Continual regeneration and sustainability happen when MTSS is adjusted based on the emerging needs of schools. After a school builds a responsive MTSS that is designed to serve all students well, they must still continually check that they are hearing from all our students, families, and community members. Anyone who has been in education for a while knows that the needs of students differ from those from even 10 years ago. Yet many schools continue to operate the same way year after year. By using data to continue to monitor and adjust for student needs, schools can strive to create systems that work for all learners.

If we return to our analogy of the recipe, then we can think of implementation science as the utensils that help all the ingredients work well together. Using the stages of implementation help you to examine the contextual factors and additional ingredients that your school or district may need. As we move into the following chapters, we will suggest guiding questions by implementation stage. How can you use the tools offered by implementation science to focus on the equity and wellness needs of your learning community?

EXAMPLE FROM THE FIELD

Johnny Phu, the director of Student Services for Lake Washington School District in Redmond, Washington, which has 57 schools serving 30,000 students, offers this advice around MTSS and implementation science.

> My biggest piece of advice is before you jump in to use the science, you start with your values. What are your values as a school or district and how might these show up when implementing MTSS, and do the values of the school or district reflect the values of your community? You also must be willing to really slow down to get everyone on the same page, even when being pushed to go fast. Lastly, I would say you really have to contextualize MTSS for your community, so this starts with knowing your community well. Once you have taken these steps, it is about following the stages

REFERENCES

Bal, A., Schrader, E. M., Afacan, K., & Mawene, D. (2016). Using learning labs for culturally responsive positive behavioral interventions and supports. *Intervention in School and Clinic, 52*, 122–128.

Eber, L., Barrett, S., Perales, K., Jeffrey-Pearsall, J., Pohlman, K., Putnam, R, Splett, J., & Weist, M. D. (2019). *Advancing education effectiveness: Interconnecting school mental health and school-wide PBIS, Volume 2: An implementation guide.* Center for Positive Behavior Interventions and Supports (funded by the Office of Special Education Programs, U.S. Department of Education). University of Oregon Press.

Fixsen, D. L., Blase, K. A., Horner, R., & Sugai, G. (2009, February). *Scaling-up evidence based practices in education.* Scaling-up Brief #1. The University of North Carolina, FPG, SISEP.

Horner, R. H., Newton, J. S., Todd, A. W., Algozzine, B., Algozzine, K., Cusumano, D., & Preston, A. (2018). A randomized waitlist controlled analysis of team-initiated problem solving professional development and use. *Behavioral Disorders, 43*, 444–456.

Kraft, M.A., Blazar, D., & Hogan, D. (2018). The effect of teaching coaching on instruction and achievement: A meta-analysis of the causal evidence. *Review of Educational Research, 88*, 547–588.

Metz, A., & Louison, L. (2018) *The hexagon tool: Exploring context*. Chapel Hill, NC: National Implementation Research Network, Frank Porter Graham Child Development Institute, University of North Carolina at Chapel Hill. Based on Kiser, Zabel, Zachik, & Smith (2007) and Blase, Kiser & Van Dyke (2013).

Metz, A., Burke, K., & Albers, B. (2020). *A practice guide to supporting implementation: What competencies do we need?* National Implementation Research Network, Frank Porter Graham Child Development Institute, University of North Carolina at Chapel Hill.

Metz, A., Woo, B., & Loper, A. (2021) Equitable implementation at work. S*tanford Social Innovation Review*, Summer Edition, 1–4.

National Implementation Research Network (2020). *Implementation stages planning tool.* Chapel Hill, NC: NIRC, FPG Child Development Institute, University of North Carolina at Chapel Hill.

Powell, B. J., Waltz T. J., Chinman, M. J., Damschroder, L. J., Smith, J. L., Matthieu, M. M., Proctor, E. K., & Kirchner, J. E. (2015). A refined compilation of implementation strategies: Results from the Expert Recommendations for Implementing Change (ERIC) Project. *Implementation Science, 10,* 21.

Safir, S., & Dugan, J. (2021). *Street data: A next-generation model for equity, pedagogy, and school transformation.* Corwin Publishing.

State Implementation and Scaling-up of Evidenced-based Practices (2023). https://sisep.fpg.unc.edu.

Todd, A.W., Horner, R. H., Newton, J. S., Algozzine, K. M., Frank, J. L., Horner R. H., Newton J. S., Todd A. W., Algozzine B., Algozzine K., Cusumano, D., & Preston, A. (2011). Effects of team-initiated problem solving on meeting practices of schoolwide behavior support teams. *Journal of Applied School Psychology, 27,* 42–59.

Chapter 4

Social Emotional Learning (SEL) and MTSS

Investing in Today and Tomorrow

WHY INVEST IN SEL?

Today's K–12 schools encompass a rich tapestry of students and staff from various racial, ethnic, cultural, linguistic, and socioeconomic backgrounds. Learning the prosocial skills needed to collaborate, grow, and play with people from a variety of backgrounds is essential in today's schools, communities, and workplaces. As mentioned in chapter 1, MTSS research and practice emphasizes the vital role of social emotional learning (SEL) in building equity and inclusion as part of schoolwide systems. Recent studies have documented how SEL interventions, when designed with cultural sensitivity and inclusivity in mind, can significantly reduce racial disparities in discipline and can create more equitable learning environments for all members of the learning community (Gregory & Fergus, 2017).

As explored in chapter 2, diversity encompasses a broad range of factors, including cultural, linguistic, and socioeconomic differences. Effective SEL implementation acknowledges and respects these differences, ensuring that SEL programs are culturally responsive and inclusive (Meyers et al., 2015). Recent research has consistently shown that when implemented intentionally, SEL is a universally applicable framework, benefiting students from diverse backgrounds. Studies by Jagers et al. (2015) and Osher et al. (2016) emphasize how effective SEL can create inclusive school cultures, reduce discipline disparities, and foster respect and empathy among students of varying racial, ethnic, and cultural backgrounds. Families express their appreciation for SEL programs that bridge cultural differences and promote belonging.

In an era when mental health problems among students are on the rise, recent studies have explored how SEL can be both a preventive and supportive measure. SEL programs that explicitly address emotional well-being and coping strategies have shown promise in reducing symptoms of anxiety and depression (Weissberg & Cascarino, 2013; Weissberg et al., 2015). Students with disabilities face unique challenges, making SEL especially crucial for their learning and well-being. Studies by McIntyre et al. (2020) and Brackett et al. (2012) reveal that SEL interventions tailored to the specific needs of students with disabilities can significantly improve their prosocial skills, self-regulation, and overall sense of emotional well-being. Such interventions contribute to more inclusive and supportive school environments.

At the same time, the world is in a constant state of change. We can now only imagine what work and social connections will look like in the future. In their report on the importance of teaching skills necessary for employment, the Business Roundtable/Change the Equation, an association of CEOs of America's leading companies that focuses on economic and public policy, found in one survey that 98% of CEOs reported that they struggle to find candidates with the competencies and training to fill their open positions. The skills cited as those most needed included effective communication, decision-making, critical thinking, problem-solving, collaboration, creativity, and innovation, all components of SEL (Committee for Children, 2016).

Employers want to hire and retain employees who think critically and work effectively with others in addition to having specific content and technical knowledge. Recent longitudinal studies reinforce the enduring benefits of SEL. They indicate that students who receive SEL instruction not only perform better academically during their school years but also exhibit improved social and emotional well-being well into adulthood (Taylor et al., 2017).

CORE SEL COMPETENCIES

The Collaborative for Academic, Social, and Emotional Learning (CASEL) is a leading organization in the field of social-emotional learning. Their SEL framework provides a comprehensive approach to the development of social and emotional skills in individuals, particularly useful in educational and work settings (2020). The CASEL framework consists of the following five core competencies that include a range of skills and attitudes necessary for positive personal and interpersonal development:

1. Self-Awareness: This competency involves the ability to recognize one's emotions, strengths, and areas for growth. It also includes cultivating a sense of self-confidence and self-efficacy. Developing self-awareness helps individuals to better understand themselves and their emotions. This can lead to improved decision-making and self-regulation.

2. Self-Management: Self-management encompasses the ability to actively regulate one's emotions, thoughts, and behaviors effectively. Examples include setting personal and academic goals and working toward meeting them, managing stress, and demonstrating perseverance and resilience in the face of challenges.
3. Social Awareness: Social awareness involves the capacity to empathize and understand the feelings, needs, and perspectives of others. This competency fosters the development of empathy, appreciation for diversity, and the ability to establish positive and respectful relationships.
4. Relationship Skills: This competency focuses on building and maintaining healthy relationships with others. It involves effective communication, active listening, cooperation, and conflict resolution skills. Developing strong relationship skills is essential for creating a positive and supportive social environment at home, in school, and at the workplace.
5. Responsible Decision-Making: Responsible decision-making refers to the ability to make constructive choices based on ethical considerations, one's social norms, and personal values. This competency includes understanding the consequences of one's actions and the ability to accept responsibility for them.

Many states, including Illinois and Washington, have used these five skills to establish SEL learning standards for their schools.

Neuroscientific studies have provided deeper insights into how SEL impacts brain development. Recent research using neuroimaging techniques highlights the neural mechanisms underlying emotional regulation and empathy development, and sheds light on the neurological basis of SEL outcomes and its relevance in K-12 schools (Braun et al., 2020). This research points to the connection between SEL, mental health, and readiness to learn.

SEL, EQUITY, AND INCLUSION

Decades of study suggest that SEL holds immense promise in culturally diverse K–12 schools, where nurturing emotional intelligence and fostering positive relationships can significantly impact both academic and social-emotional outcomes. Because SEL provides students with the intrapersonal and interpersonal skills needed to be effective learners and positive members of their learning community, it is considered an essential element of MTSS systems and supports. Indeed, CASEL describes a shared goal with MTSS: the movement toward "transformative" SEL in schools. CASEL (2020) defines transformative SEL as:

a form of SEL implementation where young people and adults build strong, respectful, and lasting relationships to engage in co-learning. It facilitates critical examination of individual and contextual factors that contribute to inequities and collaborative solutions that lead to personal, community, and societal well-being.

Reinke et al. (2018) found that integrating SEL into an MTSS framework led to improvements in students' social-emotional competence, reductions in their behavior problems, and improvements in their academic achievement. A similar study by Stormont and colleagues (2016) found that integrating SEL into an MTSS framework also improved students' social-emotional competence and reduced behavior problems, particularly for students who were at high risk for behavior problems. These and similar studies suggest that by incorporating SEL into MTSS systems and supports schools can provide all students with the social-emotional skills and support they need to be successful in school and in life.

In today's educational landscape, promoting equity and inclusion is a central focus of MTSS research and practice. For many years, much of the SEL curricula and materials found in schools have been developed and normed on populations that are limited in ethnic and gender diversity and are often implemented with limited community input. This has resulted in many students, families, and community members experiencing yet another source of marginalization and oppression as part of their school experience. Intentional, equitable, and inclusive SEL for all learners can empower students by building the skills and understanding needed to create a place of belonging and intellectual growth for every learner. MTSS provides a structure that allows all students to have equitable access to a tiered system of supports with culturally responsive and inclusive SEL at the center, strengthening their academic and behavioral development.

Zaretta Hammond, in her 2015 book *Culturally Responsive Teaching and the Brain:* Promoting Authentic Engagement and Rigor Among Culturally and Linguistically Diverse Students, writes,

> The reality is that students struggle not because of their race, language, or poverty. They struggle because we don't offer them sufficient opportunities in the classroom to develop the cognitive skills and habits of mind that would prepare them to take on more advanced academic tasks. That's the achievement gap in action.

Well planned, relevant, and inclusive SEL creates the ongoing opportunity to explicitly teach the skills and strategies needed for *all* students to be successful in learning and life. By integrating SEL with academic learning and the classroom and school climate, educators not only begin to break down the "achievement gap," they help to build resilience and a sense of belonging throughout the learning community.

SEL is also inherently linked to the effective implementation of inclusion. In diverse schools, where students may come from varied cultural backgrounds with a wide range of abilities and needs, SEL offers a common language that bridges differences. SEL programs reinforce the importance of respect, empathy, and acceptance, fostering a sense of belonging for all students, even those with disabilities, both visible and invisible (Osher et al., 2016). The Council of Chief State School Officers, in their helpful guide entitled *SEL MTSS Toolkit for State and District Leaders: Integrating Social Emotional Learning Within a Multi-Tiered Systems of Supports to Advance Equity* (2021), states,

> Through systemic SEL, SEL approaches are infused throughout every interaction and setting students encounter (Mahoney et al., 2020). MTSS is designed to help practitioners organize supports in a multilevel prevention system so that all students have what they need to succeed when they need it (Schumann et al., 2020). By integrating SEL into MTSS, education systems provide students with more of the vital opportunities to develop and apply social and emotional competencies.

SEL AND IMPROVED ACADEMIC PERFORMANCE: A STRONG CONNECTION

In a seminal 2011 study, Durlak and colleagues found that students who participated in systemic SEL gained an average of 11 percentile points on standardized tests scores compared to students who did not receive SEL. This study also found that students who received systemic SEL demonstrated:

- increased academic and SEL skills
- improved attitudes toward self and others
- improved positive social behaviors and
- decreased conduct problems and emotional distress

In diverse schools, where students may face varying levels of academic preparedness, SEL can help to level the playing field for all learners. SEL interventions have shown promise in enhancing literacy and numeracy skills. By fostering skills like active listening, collaboration, problem-solving, and effective communication, SEL contributes to improved comprehension and problem-solving abilities that are often a part of current curricula (Jones et al., 2017).

BENEFITS OF SEL FOR EDUCATORS

Along with improving outcomes for students, SEL can significantly contribute to educators' sense of efficacy and success by enhancing their teaching effectiveness and overall personal well-being. This is an important benefit of SEL as educators are leaving the profession in record numbers and those who remain in schools are still recovering from the impacts of the COVID-19 pandemic. SEL can benefit educators in the following ways:

1. Improved Classroom Management: Quality SEL materials and activities equip educators with strategies to foster a positive and inclusive classroom environment, leading to better classroom management and reduced disruptive behavior. Students who feel emotionally supported are more engaged, which in turn helps teachers maintain a focused learning atmosphere (Durlak et al., 2011).
2. Enhanced Teacher-Student Relationships: Implementing SEL principles, learning, and activities strengthens the connection between educators and students. Teachers who understand their students' emotional needs can more effectively build trust and rapport, promoting a nurturing learning environment (Jones et al., 2017).
3. Reduced Burnout and Stress: SEL training for educators helps them recognize and manage their own stress levels. By practicing self-regulation skills and self-care, educators can reduce burnout and improve their overall well-being. (Jennings & Greenberg, 2009) Studies also suggest that providing teachers with SEL training and support can reduce burnout, improve job satisfaction, and enhance their ability to create inclusive and supportive classroom environments (Jennings et al., 2017).
4. Increased Empathy and Cultural Competence: SEL fosters empathy and cultural competence among educators, enabling them to better understand and respond to the diverse needs of their students. This creates a more inclusive and equitable learning experience for every member of the learning community (Brackett et al., 2012).
5. Effective Conflict Resolution Skills: SEL equips educators with conflict resolution techniques, helping them address and resolve conflicts among students constructively. This contributes to increased feelings of belonging and cooperative learning atmosphere (Brock et al., 2019).
6. Enhanced Teaching Flexibility: Teachers who regularly practice SEL tend to be more adaptable in their instructional methods. They can better tailor their teaching approaches to accommodate different learning needs, ensuring that all students have an opportunity to succeed (Herman et al., 2018).

7. Increased Teacher Job Satisfaction: SEL implementation has been linked to higher job satisfaction among educators. When educators feel more fulfilled in their roles and observe progress in their students, they are more likely to remain in the profession and contribute positively to the school community (Oberle et al., 2016).

BRINGING SEL TO LIFE IN SCHOOLS
AND CLASSROOMS

Many schools and districts request recommendations for SEL materials and curriculum, or they are drawn to those materials that are heavily commercially promoted. It is essential that education leaders involved in making decisions about materials selection consider the alignment between materials, the backgrounds and needs of *all* members of the school or district community, and how the SEL curriculum can be integrated with existing academic and school climate initiatives. CASEL provides free curriculum guides at both the elementary and secondary levels (www.casel.org). The Wallace Foundation recently collaborated with the Harvard College of Education (Jones et al., 2021) to develop an updated guide of elementary and preschool SEL programs as well (www.wallacefoundation.org). For students with more long-standing needs or those with disabilities, the Council for Exceptional Children (CEC; www.cec.org) provides research and guidance about programs and approaches that meet the needs of students who need individualized, specially designed instruction in SEL.

With the advent of digital education, researchers are now investigating how technology can be used to deliver SEL programs effectively. Emerging research suggests that well-designed educational technology can provide accessible and impactful SEL instruction and skill development (World Economic Forum, 2016). For example, Ripple Effects, a company that develops digital SEL curriculum, is developing an SEL program that focuses on building early self-awareness and self-regulation skills for young learners. The program, called the *Bouncy Ready to Learn Resilience Program*, features an animatronic dog that teaches and models effective breath regulation in a way that makes the concept concrete and engaging for young learners. Classrooms, students, and families can practice skills and listen to favorite songs via an online application or app.

Many online applications, or apps, support teachers, students, and families in the implementation of key SEL skills. *Avokiddo* is one source for a number of online applications that offers students opportunities to practice recognizing and understanding emotions and problem-solving. Educators can also use several online games that provide opportunities for students to work together, practice, and apply the SEL skills they are learning in the context of game play. For example, the game Quandary (https://quandarygame.org /educators), provides opportunities for collaboration, problem-solving, and perspective-taking in the context of a role-playing game.

While technology can provide positive learning applications for students, we also know the dangers of too much screen time and that social media can have a negative effect on student mental health and online behavior. SEL and technology can intercept here, teaching students to be safe and good digital citizens. CASEL has collaborated with Common Sense Education, a foundation focused on developing digital literacy, to further explore the connection between teaching SEL and developing online safety and digital citizenship. They offer several free resources to schools and families on these topics (www.commonsense.org).

INTEGRATING SEL WITH ACADEMIC INSTRUCTION

Once students have developed necessary skills through intentional, equitable SEL instruction, effective teaching of SEL can be readily integrated into academic instruction across content areas. This allows students to practice SEL and to see the relevance of these skills in the context of academic and real-world experiences. This process allows educators to make the relevance of SEL clear for students, while increasing their connection with students overall.

Teachers can easily include SEL learning targets with their academic learning targets at the beginning of each lesson. This links the learning activities for the lesson with the SEL skills students will use throughout their learning. For example, a history class that is exploring the events that triggered World War I could practice active listening and perspective-taking during small and large group discussions. Edutopia, an online resource for educators (Edutopia.org), offers a powerful real-world example of this integration in their video, "Cooperative Learning Fits into the Calculation." The video follows teacher Chris Optiz as he shares how he uses SEL to deepen and expand the quality of learning in his middle school math classroom. As Mr. Optiz says in the video, the time invested in teaching these SEL skills pays off during further academic experiences. Effective SEL and effective academic instruction can strengthen and reinforce one another. This enhances engagement and points students toward key SEL skills needed for effective involvement and learning.

Incorporating SEL into content area lessons represents an opportunity to nurture students' emotional intelligence, resilience, and interpersonal skills while promoting subject mastery. The following are creative strategies educators have used to achieve this dual purpose across content areas and grade levels.

- Math: Collaborative Problem-Solving: In a high school math class, students work in small groups to solve complex problems. Besides mathematical concepts, they learn teamwork, effective communication, and conflict resolution.
- Science: Project-Based Learning: Elementary students engage in a science project where they investigate local environmental issues. This hands-on approach not only deepens scientific understanding but also encourages empathy and social awareness as they explore solutions to real-world problems.
- Language Arts: Literary Analysis and Empathy: Middle school students analyze literary characters' emotions, motivations, and relationships. This encourages self-awareness and empathy development. Students connect with characters' experiences, fostering emotional intelligence and perspective-taking.
- History: Perspective-Taking Through Debates: In a high school history class, students participate in debates about historical events. This activity nurtures social awareness and relationship skills by requiring them to understand different viewpoints and to engage in respectful dialogue.
- Physical Education: SEL Through Movement: In a kindergarten physical education class, students engage in activities that encourage self-regulation and social awareness. For example, mindful movement sessions teach them to manage emotions and consider others' feelings.
- Art: Emotional Expression: Elementary art classes incorporate SEL by having students create artwork that reflects their emotions as they listen to a variety of musical genres. This not only enhances self-awareness but also allows students to express feelings in a safe and creative way.
- Physical Education: Mindfulness Practices: High school physical education classes incorporate mindfulness exercises. Students practice self-awareness, self-regulation, and stress-reduction techniques while engaging in physical activity and learning about their developing minds and bodies.

Integrating SEL into academic learning experiences offers a rich and multifaceted approach to student centered education. SEL not only deepens understanding of subjects but also empowers students with shared, essential social-emotional skills, deepening and enriching their learning. By applying these approaches, educators can enhance student engagement, academic achievement, and overall well-being for all students.

HOW DISTRICT AND SCHOOL LEADERS
CAN SUPPORT SEL IMPLEMENTATION

While teachers bring SEL to life for their students, it is district and school leaders that build the infrastructure to support a sustainable and effective SEL initiative. School district leaders play a pivotal role in fostering the effective implementation of SEL in diverse K-12 schools, ultimately contributing to students' academic success and social-emotional well-being. The following are key steps that state, district, and school leaders must take to bring SEL to life in their systems and schools include the following:

Develop a Clear SEL Policy: School district leaders should create a comprehensive SEL policy that outlines the district's commitment to SEL, defines goals, and provides a roadmap for implementation (CASEL, 2020).

Allocate Enough Resources: Ensure that sufficient funding and resources are allocated for SEL initiatives, including professional development for educators, curriculum materials, and assessment tools (Durlak et al., 2011).

Provide Ongoing Professional Development: Offer regular, high-quality professional development opportunities for educators that equip them with the knowledge and skills needed to effectively teach SEL (Elias et al., 2015).

Foster Collaborative Learning Communities: Encourage the formation of collaborative learning communities among educators and administrators in which they can share best practices and lessons learned (Osher et al., 2016).

Promote Data-Driven Decision-Making: Emphasize the use of data to assess the impact of SEL programs and inform decision-making (Taylor et al., 2017). Regularly collect and analyze data related to SEL outcomes.

Culturally Responsive SEL Practices: Advocate for culturally responsive SEL practices that address the unique needs of diverse student populations (Jones et al., 2017).

Supportive Leadership: School district leaders should model SEL competencies and provide strong support for principals and school leaders to implement SEL initiatives (Osher et al., 2016).

Engage Parents and Communities: Involve parents and community stakeholders in SEL initiatives. Create opportunities for family engagement and community partnerships (CASEL, 2020).

Monitor and Evaluate SEL Implementation: Establish a system for monitoring and evaluating SEL implementation across schools within the district. Use this data to identify areas for improvement and share successful strategies (Taylor et al., 2017).

Align SEL with Academic Goals: Ensure that SEL goals are aligned with academic goals and standards. SEL should be integrated into the curriculum to reinforce its importance (CASEL, 2020).

Provide Clear Communication: Communicate the district's commitment to equitable, inclusive SEL clearly and consistently to all stakeholders. Transparency and regular updates are crucial for success (Durlak et al., 2011).

Establish a Sustainable SEL Culture: Promote a sustainable SEL culture within the district, emphasizing that SEL is an ongoing commitment, not a one-time initiative (Jones et al., 2017).

Implementing SEL effectively is not a quick process. Like all meaningful changes in systems practices, it takes time, intention, and careful planning. There is so much on the plates of educators and school leaders that it is easy to become caught up in marketing and promises of easy answers. By working through these steps, district leaders ensure that efforts to improve schools are equitable, inclusive, and sustainable. It is a worthwhile investment in the collective futures of students, families, and educators.

CONCLUSION

SEL has the potential to help transform educational settings by promoting holistic student development, addressing issues of equity and inclusion, and nurturing emotionally intelligent and academically successful learners. However, effective implementation relies on collaborative efforts from educators, administrators, families, and communities, guided by research-based practices. Investing the time and resources needed to implement SEL in schools and districts provides clear benefits to students, educators, and families. It is essential to ensure that any SEL initiative is inclusive and equitable for *all* learners. This means that schools and district must be thoughtful and intentional in implementing an SEL initiative. The implementation framework presented in table 4.1 outlines the steps that need to be taken to successfully implement an SEL initiative.

Table 4.1. Stages of Implementation Applied to SEL Initiatives

Implementation Stages	*SEL Practices Application*
Exploration—Identify the need for change, compare possible approaches to achieve change, and assess readiness for change.	Explore what approach to SEL is the best match for your school or district. Use tools from CASEL and the Wallace Foundation to identify program that might be a good match for your community. Reach out to families and community members for input on needs and potential supports. Ensure that equity and inclusivity of *all* learners, educators, and families is embedded in the initiative.
Installation—Identify the needed supports to put the practice in place with good fidelity. Gather feedback from those who will be affected.	Identify what training and supports staff need to learn to implement the SEL program with fidelity and confidence. How does your SEL approach integrate with your existing academic initiatives? What goals and measurable outcomes for this effort have been identified? What policies and practices need to be changed to support SEL across your system? How will you bring students, families, and community on board for the initiative?
Initial Implementation—Initial training, coaching, and data review supports the new skills and practices and improvement in implementation.	Adoption and alignment of SEL into the larger MTSS framework within the school or district. Staff members are trained and actively engaged in the practices. There is clear communication about the practices with families and students. Assessment of the fidelity of implementation and collection of related outcomes data is ongoing.
Full Implementation—The innovation is well-integrated into the daily practice and routines. It remains in place through administrative changes.	All staff are implementing SEL, and there is a deep connection between SEL and academic learning experiences. Students and families are actively engaged as co-learners in the implementation process.

EXAMPLE FROM THE FIELD

Parkview Elementary is located in Bellingham Public Schools in Bellingham, Washington. This suburban K–5 elementary school also includes several classrooms that support students with significant disabilities. The school has recently been expanding efforts to increase inclusion schoolwide. For the past several years, each classroom in Parkview begins their day with a class-wide circle to check in, learn new SEL skills, and get oriented for the day. The teachers use the Caring Schools Community materials to guide implementation of their circles (www.collaborativeclassroom.org).

For many years, students in the specialized classrooms participated in SEL lessons in their special education classrooms, joining their general education classrooms once circle was over. The rationale was that these students needed more in-depth lessons than provided in the general education classroom.

Last year, the school leadership team worked with general and special education teachers to shift that approach. Now, every student assigned to a classroom participates in opening circle, with push-in support from special education staff when needed. When additional SEL specially designed instruction is needed, that is scheduled at another time in the day. The team's thinking now is that students with intensive, individualized needs need *more* opportunities to learn and practice SEL, not less. Since the circle sets the tone for the day and builds belonging across the community, it is important that all students participate. Special and general education are finding that this small but powerful change sets all students in the classroom up for a more successful day. Students who need to leave the general education classroom for specially designed instruction or language supports report feeling more connected to the classroom and "not just a visitor."

REFERENCES

Brackett, M. A., Rivers, S. E., & Salovey, P. (2012). Emotional intelligence: Implications for personal, social, academic, and workplace success. *Social and Personality Psychology Compass, 6*(1), 88–103.

Braun, S.S., Schonert-Reichl, K.A., & Roser, R. (2020). Effects of teachers' emotion regulation, burnout, and life satisfaction on student well-being. *Journal of Applied Developmental Psychology, 69.* doi: 10.1016/j.appdev.2020.101151.

Brock, L. L., Nishida, T. K., Chiong, C., Grimm, K. J., & Rimm-Kaufman, S. E. (2019). Children's perceptions of teacher social-emotional responsiveness: Associations with children's feelings about school and learning. *Journal of School Psychology, 72,* 1–17.

Business Roundtable. (n.d.). *Closing the skills gap.* http://businessroundtable.org/issue-hub/closing-the-skills-gap.

Collaborative for Academic, Social, and Emotional Learning (CASEL). (2020). *What is SEL?* https://casel.org/what-is-sel/.

Collaborative for Academic, Social, and Emotional Learning (CASEL). (n.d.) *Transformative SEL.* https://casel.org/fundamentals-of-sel/how-does-sel-support-educational-equity-and-excellence/transformative-sel/.

Collaborative Classroom. (n.d.). www.collaborativeclassroom.org/programs/caring-school-community/.

Committee for Children. (2016). *Why social emotional learning and employability skills should be prioritized in education.* www.cfchildren.org/wp-content/uploads/policy-advocacy/sel-employability-brief.pdf.

Common Sense Education (in collaboration with CASEL). (n.d.). www.commonsense
.org/education/digital-citizenship/curriculum.

Council of Chief State School Officers. (2021). *The SEL MTSS Toolkit for state and district leaders: Integrating social emotion learning withing a multi-tiered system of supports to advance equity.* https://learning.ccsso.org/social-and-emotional
-learning-and-multi-tiered-system-of-supports.

Durlak, J. A., Weissberg, R. P., Dymnicki, A. B., Taylor, R. D., & Schellinger, K. B. (2011). The impact of enhancing students' social and emotional learning: A meta☐ analysis of school☐based universal interventions. *Child Development, 82*(1), 405–432.

Edutopia. "Cooperative Learning Fits into the Calculation" (video). (n.d.) www
.edutopia.org/math-social-activity-sel.

Elias, M. J., Leverett, L., Duffell, J., Humphrey, N., Stepney, C., & Ferrito, J. (2015). Implementing social and emotional learning policies in schools: A framework for schoolwide implementation. *Cambridge Journal of Education, 45*(3), 277–297.

Gregory, A., & Fergus, E. (2017). Social and emotional learning and equity in school discipline. *The Future of Children 27*(1), 117–136. doi: 10.1353/foc.2017.0006

Hammond, Z. (2015). *Culturally responsive teaching and the brain: Promoting authentic engagement and rigor among culturally and linguistically diverse students.* Corwin Press.

Herman, K. C., Hickmon-Rosa, J. P., & Reinke, W. M. (2018). Empirically derived profiles of teacher stress, burnout, self-efficacy, and coping and associated student outcomes. *Journal of Positive Behavior Interventions, 20*(2), 90–100.

Jagers, R. J., Harris, A. L., & Skoog, A. (2015). Social and emotional learning and equity in school discipline. *Children & Schools, 37*(2), 71–78.

Jennings, P. A., & Greenberg, M. T. (2009). The prosocial classroom: Teacher social and emotional competence in relation to student and classroom outcomes. *Review of educational research, 79*(1), 491–525.

Jennings, P. A., Brown, J. L., Frank, J. L., Doyle, S., Oh, Y., Davis, R., Rasheed, D., DeWeese, A., DeMauro, A. A., Cham, H., & Greenberg, M. T. (2017). Impacts of the CARE for teachers program on teachers' social and emotional competence and classroom interactions. *Journal of Educational Psychology, 109*(7), 1010–1028. doi: 10.1037/edu0000187.

Jones, S. M., Bailey, R., Barnes, S. P., & Partee, A. (2017). *Implementing social and emotional learning: A guide for school leaders.* Center on Great Teachers and Leaders.

Jones, S. M., Brush, K. E., Ramirez, T., Mao, Z. X., Marenus, M., Wettie, S., Finney, K., Raisch, N., Podoloff, N., Kahn, J., Barnes, S., Stickle, L., Brion-Meisels, G., McIntyre, J., Cuartas, J., & Bailey, R. (2021). *Navigating social emotional learning from the inside out: Looking inside and across 33 leading SEL programs, preschool and elementary focus.* Harvard Graduate School of Education. www
.wallacefoundation.org/knowledge-center/pages/navigating-social-and-emotional
-learning-from-the-inside-out.aspx.

Mahoney, J. L., Weissberg, R. P., Greenberg, M. T., Dusenbury, L., Jagers, R. J., Niemi, K., Schlinger, M., Schlund, J., Shriver, T. P., VanAusdal, K., Yoder, N.

(2021). Systemic social and emotional learning: Promoting educational success for all preschool to high school students. *American Psychologist, 76*(7), 1128–42.

McIntyre, L. L., Eckert, T. L., Fiese, B. H., DiGennaro Reed, F. D., & Wildenger, L. K. (2020). A mixed-method examination of the validity of a social-emotional learning intervention for young children with disabilities. *Early Childhood Research Quarterly, 51,* 126–138.

Meyers, D. C., Domitrovich, C. E., & Greenberg, & M. T. (2015). *The CASEL guide to effective social and emotional learning programs: Preschool and elementary school edition.* Collaborative for Academic, Social, and Emotional Learning.

Oberle, E., Domitrovich, C. E., Meyers, D. C., & Weissberg, R. P. (2016). Establishing systemic social and emotional learning approaches in schools: A framework for schoolwide implementation. *Cambridge Journal of Education, 46*(3), 277–297.

Osher, D., Kidron, Y., Brackett, M. A., Dymnicki, A., Jones, S., & Weissberg, R. P. (2016). Advancing the science and practice of social and emotional learning: Looking back and moving forward. *Review of Research in Education, 40*(1), 644–681.

Reinke, W. M., Herman, K. C., & Dong, N. (2018). The impact of integrated school-based social-emotional learning and literacy instruction on student outcomes. *School Psychology Review, 47*(2), 196–214.

Schumann, J., Rose, T., Collins, K., & Koehler, K. (2020). MTSS: A Research-based System to Ensure Equity and Access for Learning. *IARCOS Triannual Journal,* Winter 2020, 36–38. https://issuu.com/earcosorg/docs/et-winter-2020/38.

Stormont, M., Reinke, W. M., Herman, K. C., Lembke, E. S., & Darney, D. (2016). Integrating social-emotional learning with multi-tiered systems of support: Practices and perspectives of school-based professionals. *School Mental Health, 8*(2), 165–178.

Taylor, R. D., Oberle, E., Durlak, J. A., & Weissberg, R. P. (2017). Promoting positive youth development through school-based social and emotional learning interventions: A meta-analysis of follow-up effects. *Child Development, 88*(4), 1156–1171.

Wallace Foundation. (n.d.). www.wallacefoundation.org/knowledge-center/pages/navigating-social-and-emotional-learning-from-the-inside-out.aspx.

Weissberg, R. P., & Cascarino, J. (2013). Academic learning + social-emotional learning = national priority. *Phi Delta Kappan, 94*(8), 62–65.

Weissberg, R. P., Durlak, J. A., Domitrovich, C. E., & Gullotta, T. P. (eds.). (2015). *Handbook of social and emotional learning: Research and practice.* Guilford Publications.

World Economic Forum. (2016). *The future of jobs: Employment, skills and workforce strategy for the fourth industrial revolution.* www3.weforum.org/docs/WEF_Future_of_Jobs.pdf.

Chapter 5

Cultivating a Culture of Equity and Belonging with Restorative Justice Practices

WHAT ARE RESTORATIVE JUSTICE PRACTICES?

While the use of restorative justice practices (RJPs) has a relatively short history in our school systems, the practices and philosophies that constitute RJP are in harmony with many Indigenous communities worldwide, including, for example, Ojibwe, Tlingit, and Navajo peacemaking circles; the ubuntu communitarian approach found in many southern African traditions; and in the Maori community living traditions.

While many definitions of RJP exist, the one offered here is "Restorative justice practices creates a community-focused learning environment in which everyone (adults and youth) feels like they are seen, heard and valued" (Lynass & Frodge, 2018). RJP is changing from a promising practice into an evidenced-based practice in schools as it is further used and researched within the school setting. Applying MTSS logic to restorative practices causes educators to start with a prevention-first stance. Using restorative practices, this prevention is achieved through the intentional development and nurturing of healthy relationships.

In *The Little Book of Restorative Justice in Education*, Evans and Vaandering (2016) present three interconnected components of restorative justice in education (RJE):

- Nurturing healthy relationships
- Creating just and equitable learning environments
- Repairing harm and transforming conflict.

These three components build upon each other, starting with nurturing healthy relationships. Once an educator has established and nurtured healthy relationships with their students, they can use the information they learn to support students both academically and behaviorally. Incorporating students' prior knowledge, interests, culture, and learning styles helps us to build more just and equitable learning environments. We can then use RJP as a tool to transform conflict. Conflict is going to occur when we have large groups of people together, like in schools, and conflict can be healthy. Educators must realize that they cannot successfully repair harm and transform conflict without the focus on the other two components.

Schools often mistakenly consider restorative practices only as a tool to be used in place of traditional punishment approaches to rule violations, instead of a tool for community connection. Restorative practices cause educators to realize that what they are repairing is a broken relationship, but they can only successfully repair a relationship that has been built. When educators take the time to build relationships, they can improve their understanding of students' cultural values and their needs. This understanding also helps educators to examine their own biases that may be affecting their work in schools.

By using restorative practices, schools can address the underlying needs of those who make up the learning community. Without the dialogue that restorative practices create, educators may not be aware of what those needs really are. Addressing those needs creates more just and equitable learning environments.

To create a community-focused learning environment means that adults promote and model an ethos of care and support. This is done by examining the ways the physical and emotional environments are set up to promote this ethos of care (Amstutz & Mullet, 2015). It is also accomplished when educators commit to the values that ground RJP. In table 5.1, Brown (2018) views these values from the lenses of overarching, individual, and process values.

RESTORATIVE PRACTICES, EQUITY, AND SOCIAL TRANSFORMATION

Restorative practices challenge educational systems to dismantle the many structures, policies, and systems that contribute to the systemic and institutional racism so prevalent in the United States today. The increase in the use of zero tolerance policies after the mass shootings at Westside Middle School in Jonesboro, Arkansas in 1998 and Columbine High School in Columbine, Colorado in 1999 put more pressure on schools to criminalize youth behavior with mandatory punishments. Schools that adopt this punishment framework

Table 5.1. Overarching, Individual, and Process Restorative Justice Values

Overarching Values	Individual Values	Process Values
Empowerment	Respect	Respect
Honesty	Honesty	Individual Dignity
Respect	Compassion	Inclusion
Engagement	Open-mindedness	Responsibility
Voluntarism	Patience	Humility
Healing		Mutual Care
Restoration		Reparation
Personal Accountability		Non-denomination
Inclusiveness		
Collaboration		
Problem-Solving		

From Brown (2018); adapted from Morrison (2007) and Pranis (2006)

have often seen an increase, rather than a decrease, in discipline issues (Skiba & Losen, 2015).

While already widely used in countries such as New Zealand and Australia, the use of restorative practices to transform exclusionary discipline was propelled ahead in the United States by the Obama administration in a 2014 "Dear College" letter jointly written by the U.S. Department of Education and the U.S. Department of Justice Civil Right Division. With suspensions and expulsions impacting students who are Black, Indigenous, and People of Color (BIPOC) at disproportionate rates, students have been pushed out of schools by the use of punishment and exclusion.

In support of RJP as a tool to change our school environments, Fania Davis (2019) writes:

> For more than five hundred years, Western knowledge systems based on an ethos of separateness, competition, and subordination have contributed to pervasive crises that today imperil our future. The unfathomable magnitude of destruction has fueled a quest for alternative worldviews that bring healing to our world. It is in this historical context we witness the rapid rise and spread of restorative justice.

CORE PRACTICES IN RJP

RJP as used in schools is built upon four core premises or philosophies. The first underlying premise of RJP is the Social Discipline Window, which illustrates that people are more likely to engage and feel their needs are being met when those in authority are making decisions and doing things *with* them rather than *for* or *to* them (Costello et al., 2010). This helps educators to reach a balance between a physical and emotional ethos of care, as represented in figure 5.1.

From figure 5.1 we can see that when school staff have a balance that has high expectations and control but also has the needed encouragement and support, they operate in the *with* quadrant. If we think of these quadrants as classrooms, we have highly cooperative learning activities, student-led learning, and shared accountability. In the *to* quadrant, staff are focused heavily on control, but they lack the needed support. In the *for* quadrant, staff have high levels of support but lack the needed control and high expectations, and in the *not* quadrant, staff lack both control and nurturing leading to a classroom that feels chaotic and unsafe. The Social Discipline Window is an important tool to help staff examine how they structure learning to best promote this ethos of care.

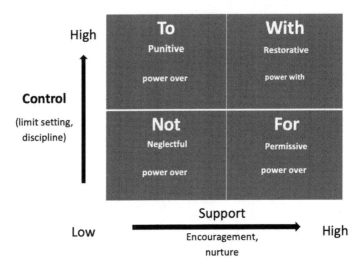

Figure 5.1. Social Discipline Window

The second underlying premise of RJP is the use of a concept called *fair process*. The idea of fair process comes from a 1997 article by Kim and Mauborgne that highlights how trust and cooperation can be built when people feel they have a voice in the decision-making process, making that process fair. This is true regardless of whether the outcome is the one that the person wanted. Kim and Mauborgne propose that to create this process, three principles of the decision-making must exist:

1. Engagement—Involving those in the decision-making process who are affected by it and allowing them to contest each other's ideas, creating a dialogue that allows for various perspectives to be shared.
2. Explanation—Providing to those affected by the decision an explanation about how and why the final decision was made. This creates the needed feedback loop about the process.
3. Expectation clarity—Once a decision is made, making the new expectations related to that decision clear, so they are understood. This may include changes in policies or procedures.

The third underlying premise is the use of circle practices to both build community and address issues. The majority of circles that are run in a school should be prevention-based and focused on building a positive school climate. This is done by using circles as a tool to check in, share perspectives and values, make connections, and improve academic dialogue.

When used to address behavior, restorative practices move away from the use of punishment and instead takes a discipline approach in which persons affected by actions discuss what happened and how to make things as right as possible. This is a shift that moves from examining the rule that was broken to focusing on the harm done to relationships and the consequent needs. When schools focus on a restorative approach to discipline, they also focus on building the systems that allow behavioral errors to be addressed in a way that strengthens relationships and gives everyone involved a voice in the process.

Circles focused on repairing harm have three phases to address the issue. The first phase is to establish what happened. Those in the circle may not agree on what happened, but it is important that everyone's perspectives be shared. The second phase is to share the impacts that resulted from the incident from each person's viewpoint. Again, in this phase participants don't have to agree on the impacts. The goal is to raise awareness about how each person in the circle and any others may have been impacted. The third phase is to then establish what needs to happen to allow those impacted and those who caused the impact to make things as right as possible.

These three phases are then achieved by following a set circle process that often involves some variation of the following questions:

- What happened?
- What were you thinking at the time?
- What have you thought about since?
- Who has been affected and in what ways?
- What do you think needs to be done to make things right?

This set of questions is intended to be more open-ended and non-judgmental. The goal in this process is to build more introspection and self-awareness about the actions taken and resulting harm that has occurred. Generally, when talking about harm occurring, people are talking about the relationships and trust that have been harmed.

A relationship must exist in the first place to be repaired. When that relationship does not exist, people have less care about how their actions impact others. Once a circle has been run and the parties involved have decided what actions will make things right, there should be follow-up that occurs to make sure that the agreed upon actions did occur. It is suggested that in the repair circle a process like a circle agreements sheet is used to write down the agreements made and to document who will be following up to make sure those agreements were met.

The fourth underlying premise when using RJP in schools is student engagement and the ways that educators authentically partner with youth in these practices. Student engagement is central to the process of building learning environments that are just and equitable. More than ever, young people are demonstrating agency by asking to have a voice in their educational journey.

The positive impacts of RJP on school culture cannot be fully obtained and sustained in schools until youth are authentically engaged in having shared ownership of the work. Aquino et al. (2019) define youth engagement in restorative justice as "meaningful participation of youth who are most impacted by structural injustice as changemakers and practitioners in all aspects of restorative justice including community building, healing and the transformation of self and institutions."

HOW TO GET STARTED

Schools interested in implementing restorative practices should invest in adequate training for all staff. It is suggested that students be exposed to circles for building community on a regular basis before being engaged in a harm circles process. Therefore, all staff will need training in running proactive circles. While not all staff will run the harm and repair circles, they should all understand the format and purpose of the use of these circles versus the use of traditional punishment. If a school rushes into using RJP only as a tool to address discipline, they will likely set themselves up for failure.

Implementation should be thought of as a marathon rather than a sprint. Using the implementation science logic discussed in chapter 3, educators can think about implementation across the four stages. Table 5.2 shows this implementation as it applies to RJP.

Table 5.2. Stages of Implementation Applied to Restorative Justice Practices

Implementation Stages	*Restorative Justice Practices (RJPs) Application*
Exploration—Identify the need for change, compare possible approaches to achieve change, and assess readiness for change.	Explore if RJPs will help you bring about the desired change(s). Use tools such as readiness assessments, speaking with other schools and training to explore readiness. What needs within the school will RJPs address?
Installation—Identify the supports needed to put the practice in place with good fidelity. Gather feedback from those who will be affected.	What are the systems that need to be built to assure restorative justice practices can be implemented with high fidelity? What measurable outcomes goals have been identified? What policies and practices need to be changed to support RJPs being installed?
Initial Implementation—Provide the initial training, coaching, and data review that supports the new skills, practices, and improvement in implementation.	RJPs are adopted into and aligned with the larger MTSS framework within the school. Staff members are trained and actively engaged in the practices. There is clear communication about the practices with families and students. Assessment of the fidelity of implementation and collection of related outcomes data is ongoing.
Full Implementation—The innovation is well-integrated into the daily practice and routines. It remains in place through administrative changes.	All staff are implementing restorative practices, and youth are actively engaged as co-facilitators in the implementation process.

A readiness assessment can help with the first phase of exploration. It should be completed by the MTSS team and include input from all interested parties involved. A link to a suggested readiness assessment can be found in chapter 8. Once the implementation has begun, schools should measure the fidelity of implementation. A fidelity tool from Swain-Bradway, et al. (2019) can be found on the Sound Supports page under resources and can help guide the implementation process.

Once a school is ready to truly create a restorative environment, the circle practice should start with staff. Invested staff should hold circles together to build community and strengthen their own practice. However, it is also important to actively engage the youth in the school in RJP early in the process. Remember that youth can be strong agents of change in helping educators examine ways current policies and practices are harming rather than helping them. How do restorative practices fit into your recipe for MTSS, and how can you use table 5.2 as a guide?

EXAMPLE FROM THE FIELD

The Kent School District MTSS Team in Kent, Washington, has focused on expanding their work with restorative practices since initial training. One of the MTSS coaches stated, "We found that coming back to our first full year from COVID, we really had to focus on the staff and rebuild the connections they needed with each other. Many of the staff had felt very isolated during COVID and were having a hard time collaborating well together. We had Lori Lynass lead a circle with staff at a school that were struggling to connect. Many staff admitted that they did not even know everyone's names from staff changes that occurred during COVID."

One of the district's goals for the current school year is to take over classrooms and relieve the teacher for 30 minutes, so they can run either one-on-one or small-group circles focused on getting to know their students better. The MTSS team will initially model for them how to do these circles. The team will focus initially on those grades transitioning from elementary school to middle school or middle school to high school. Modeling circles and modeling SEL lessons for teachers has really helped to lay the foundation.

REFERENCES

Amstutz, L. S., & Mullet, J. H. (2015). *The little book of restorative discipline for schools: Teaching responsibility and creating caring climates.* Good Books Publishing.

Aquino, E., Manchester H. B., & Wadwha, A. (2019). *The little book of youth engagement in restorative justice: Intergenerational partnerships for just and equitable schools.* Good Books Publishing.

Brown, M. A. (2018), *Creating restorative school: Setting schools up to succeed.* Living Justice Press.

Costello, B., Wachtel, J., & Wachtel, T. (2010). *Restorative circles in schools: Building community and enhancing learning.* International Institute of Restorative Practices.

Davis, F. (2019). *The little book of race and restorative justice.* Good Books Publishing.

Evans, K., & Vaandering, D. (2016). *The little book of restorative justice in education.* Good Books Publishing,

Kim, W.C., & Mauborne, R. (1997). Fair process: Managing in the knowledge economy. *Harvard Business Review, 75,* 65–75.

Lynass, L., & Frodge, C. (2018). *Restorative justice practices for schools training workbook.* Sound Supports. www.soundsupportsk12.com.

Morrison, B. E. (2007). *Restoring safe school communities: A whole school response to bullying, violence and alienation.* The Federation Press.

Pranis, K. (2006). Restorative values. In Johnston, G., & Van Ness, D. W. *Handbook of restorative justice*. Willan Publishing.

Skiba, R. J., & Losen, D. J. (2015). From reaction to prevention: Turning the page on school discipline. *American Educator, 39*, 4–11.

Swain-Bradway, J., Eber, L., Johnson, Hearn, A., Balgoyen, S., & Maggin, J. (2019). *Restorative practices in school-wide PBIS fidelity implementation checklist.* Sound Supports. www.soundsupportsk12.com.

Chapter 6

Implementing School-Based Mental Health in the MTSS Framework

THE NEED FOR INTEGRATED SCHOOL-BASED MENTAL HEALTH SUPPORTS

The mental health of students impacts how they think, feel, and behave and determines how well they handle stress and at what level they can participate in learning. It is estimated that 20% of school-aged children and youth need some type of mental health intervention, but the research tells us that only about 30% of those students actually receive services. Of those who do receive services, about 70% receive them at school (CDC, 2017).

Schools can play a critical role in protecting students' mental health by promoting student health and development in the climate that schools create. This environment must be intentionally designed to be a place where all students feel seen, heard, valued, and cared for. The MTSS framework is designed to help create that climate of acceptance and belonging.

There has been a recent increase in mental health concerns in young people. This most commonly manifests in depression, withdrawal, anxiety, and somatic symptoms (Mojtabai & Olfson, 2020). According to the data from the 2021 Youth Risk Behavior Survey (YRBS), more than 40% of high school students reported feeling so sad or hopeless that they could not engage in regular activities for at least a two-week span during the previous year (CDC, 2021). The data also showed a significant increase in the percentage of youth who had seriously considered suicide, created a suicide plan, or attempted suicide. The disaggregated data indicated that 60% of female students in 2021 experienced persistent feelings of hopelessness or sadness and nearly

25% of them had made a suicide plan. This data reporting feeling sad or hopeless rose to 70% for the LGBQ+ population (CDC, 2021).

This is not a new issue. Analysis of the YRBS data from 2015 showed that high school students who had A, B, and C grades were more likely to report having more health-related protective factors and a lower prevalence of health-related risk behaviors than their peers who had D or F grades (CDC, 2021). In addition to impacting school performance, mental health issues and chronic levels of stress can have other short-term and lifelong effects. The corresponding poor outcomes that result when mental health needs go untreated contribute to an increase in adolescents engaging in substance abuse and being identified as at risk for suicide (CDC, 2021).

Experiences of racism in schools have impacted the mental wellness of students of color. According to the CDC (2021), perceived racism was highest among students who identified as Asian (67.9%), Black (62.1%), or Hispanic/Latinx (45.7). Experiences of racism can affect students' feelings of safety while at school. This is a health-related factor that must be explicitly addressed in the school environment. Hispanic and Black students were more likely than Asian, White, and multiracial students to not attend school due to safety concerns. Racial discrimination in schools affects both academic achievement and educational attainment (Tobler et al., 2013).

Exposure to ongoing stress has a real impact on child and adolescent development. Research from the Harvard Center on the Developing Child (2023) shows chronic stress can be toxic to the developing brain. This is due to the brain becoming flooded with cortisol, which is produced when someone feels anxious or stressed. In the youngest learners, chronic stress and adverse childhood experiences inhibit healthy neurological pathways from developing.

Exposure to chronic stress can also cause the brain's prefrontal cortex to shrink, which can impair memory and learning. Chronic stress can also increase the size of the amygdala, which are responsible for the flight, fight, or freeze responses (McEwan, 2016). This means that students experiencing chronic stress may be more likely to have responses like leaving the classroom or refusing to go to school (flight), aggressive or combative behaviors (fight), or disengagement or anxiety (freeze).

The good news is that when the source of the chronic stress is effectively addressed, the young, developing brain can bounce back and grow new neural pathways. This is referred to as neuroplasticity, which means that these changes do not have to be permanent (McEwan, 2016). When a consistent and predictable learning environment that nurtures relationships is provided, students relax, and their cortisol levels are reduced. Activities such as positive interactions, physical activity, and mindfulness are easily deliverable in the school setting at a tier 1 level and can greatly support all students.

BARRIERS TO ACCESSING MENTAL
HEALTH SUPPORTS IN SCHOOLS

Despite having knowledge about poor student outcomes being related to mental health issues, schools still struggle to deliver the needed mental health care efficiently and effectively. As Barrett et al. (2023) state, "This public health crisis is a whole population response." This response must bring schools and communities together to meet the needs of youth more efficiently. There are real barriers that play a significant role in whether children can access the needed support. In a report examining the mental health crisis impacting students, the U.S. Department of Education (2021) identified these barriers to accessing needed support:

- perceived stigma in needing mental health support
- ineffective implementation practices
- fragmented delivery systems
- policy and funding gaps
- gaps in professional development and support
- lack of access to usable data to guide implementation decision

As previously noted, research indicates that most students who receive some type of mental health services do so at school (CDC, 2017). This makes sense since students spend a large majority of their waking day in school. The challenge for schools and educators has become how to assure that all students who need support are able to access it. One positive aspect for schools is that the research and knowledge about how to help mitigate mental health issues has increased in the past decade.

HOW TO INTEGRATE SCHOOL-BASED MENTAL
HEALTH SUPPORTS INTO THE MTSS FRAMEWORK

The purpose of the MTSS framework is to streamline the approach to the delivery of services, including mental health supports. Schools are often trying to run several teams and committees focused on multiple initiatives, which does not work well. In many schools already implementing positive and behavioral interventions and supports (PBIS), the mental health supports are separate and siloed, and frequently provided by outside agencies coming into the school on a contract basis. These factors prevent schools from serving a higher number of students effectively.

According to Flaherty and Osher (2003), the history of supporting the mental health of students within schools can be traced back to the Progressive Era (1896–1917). It was during this era that many of the disciplines such as school psychologist, school counselor, and school social worker were developed. The 1980s brought mental health support from the community into many schools to serve more students who otherwise would not access needed support (Flaherty & Osher, 2003).

Another national effort to bring more mental health services into schools came under the *Now Is the Time Initiative* (White House, 2013), championed by then-President Barack Obama, which included funding for several school-based initiatives including the Safe Schools/Healthy Students Initiative, Project Prevent, Project AWARE, and the School Climate Transformation grants (The White House, 2013). In response to the COVID-19 pandemic, the Elementary and Secondary Schools Emergency Relief funding (ESSER) also became temporarily available to support efforts (Office of Elementary and Secondary Education, 2020).

The most recent funding supports have come from the 2022 *Bipartisan Safer Communities Act,* which promotes access to school mental health services. Integrating mental health supports into a school's MTSS framework is necessary to achieve the efficiency needed to serve multiple students. This increased access is about equity, because many students that do not access mental health support are students of color and students from low-income backgrounds.

When addressing trauma and mental health needs, early intervention is always more effective. Research shows that the longer educators wait to provide interventions the less likely they are to be successful (Colizzi et al., 2020). Prevention science has taught educators that supports must be implemented that begin at tier 1 and are available for all students and staff. Examples supports at tier 1 are a schoolwide focus on relationship building, and social-emotional learning that is focused on providing the needed social skills and strategies to cope with the daily stress that many students experience.

Practices such as mindfulness, yoga, and other stress management strategies can be used at a tier 1 level by staff and students who are experiencing anxiety and/or stress. This teaches students that mental health supports are part of daily wellness that everyone needs to focus on. Educators must model and build a culture in schools that embraces mental health services as truly being for all members of the community.

Within the MTSS framework, many districts and schools are using the Interconnected Systems Framework (ISF) to meet students' mental health needs more efficiently and effectively (Eber et al., 2019). ISF provides schools with both a structure and a process to design and deliver a single system of supports across both education and mental health with an emphasis on family and youth engagement. Eber et al. (2019) stated "the overall purpose of such an integrated system is to create a school culture and climate that promotes wellness of the whole child and addresses the needs of all students especially those at risk for or with mental health challenges."

ISF uses the three-tiered logic of MTSS to continually look at ways to prevent and intervene early with mental health needs. Four key messages can be found in the ISF (Eber et al., 2019). In summary these are:

1. A single system of delivery is necessary.
2. Mental health is for all.
3. Access alone is not enough.
4. MTSS is essential to install School-Based Mental Health.

Aligning with MTSS, Splett et al. (2019) identify the core features of ISF as:

- implementation of school-wide PBIS
- teaming
- collaborative planning and training
- family and youth engagement
- intervention selection, implementation, and progress
- school-wide data-based decision-making

Fortunately, the information about implementing ISF is available free to all schools because of a generous partnership between The National Technical Assistance Center on PBIS, The United States Office of Special Education Programs (OSEP), and the Substance Abuse and Mental Health Services Administration (SAMHSA). Because these resources are freely available, it is not necessary to go into detail here about how to implement the ISF. In-depth resources about ISF can be found at the National PBIS Technical Assistance website (www.pbis.org).

ROLE OF THE LEADERS IN INTEGRATING SMH INTO THE MTSS FRAMEWORK

A great place to start this work is with the logic of the implementation science framework introduced in chapter 3. This framework reminds us that effective implementation is a multi-year process that begins with exploration. Table 6.1 at the end of this chapter contains guiding questions for each stage

Table 6.1. Stages of Implementation Applied to School Mental Health and the Interconnected Systems Framework

Implementation Stages	School Mental Health Application
Exploration—Identify the need for change, compare possible approaches to achieve change, and assess readiness for change.	Have we clearly identified the need for SMH support through a needs assessment? What mental health supports are in place now? What is our current level of readiness for change? Do we have a representative team in place to guide this work? Do we have a shared core understanding of the Interconnected Systems Framework (ISF)?
Installation—Identify the needed supports to put the practice in place with good fidelity. Gather feedback from those who will be affected.	What are the systems that need to be built to assure that the ISF can be implemented with strong fidelity? What measurable outcomes goals have been identified? What policies and practices need to be changed to support SMH being installed?
Initial Implementation—Initial training and coaching and data review supports the new skills, practices, and improvement in implementation.	SMH practices are adopted into and aligned with the larger MTSS framework within the school. Staff members are trained in the ISF framework and actively engaged in the work. There is clear communication about the integration of SMH with families and students. Assessment of the fidelity of implementation and collection of related outcomes data is ongoing.
Full Implementation—The innovation is well-integrated into the daily practice and routines and remains in place through administrative changes.	All staff have a role in implementing SMH. SMH practices are integrated into written policies and procedures. Funding to maintain an ISF is secured.

of implementation that can help leaders assess their schools' present status and plan to further develop those supports.

A strong and representative leadership team is essential to carry out the implementation of an ISF or integrate more School Mental Health (SMH) into the current MTSS. The team should refer to the Aligning Teaming Structures process discussed in the Introduction and look for ways to bring in SMH as a focus area of your existing MTSS team, instead of creating another new team. Community-based mental health providers who may be providing support to students and family members should be included as part of the membership of this team.

Once a team is established, the ISF School Installation Guide can provide a school team with step-by-step action items to begin the installation process. This free tool is meant to be completed by the leadership team with the guidance of a facilitator or coach who is knowledgeable about ISF. A link to the full ISF Installation Guide can be downloaded from the National PBIS Technical Assistance website (www.pbis.org), along with several additional resources for this process.

A second tool that the leadership team may consider using is the *ISF Implementation Inventory* (Splett et al., 2019) which helps school teams monitor the fidelity of the ISF implementation in schools. This free tool can be an essential part of a team's installation and progress monitoring and can be downloaded from the National PBIS Technical Assistance Center (www.pbis.org). Tools such as these can help a leadership team to implement SMH services in a systematic fashion. Remember that it is essential that the leadership team meaningfully involve the voices of students, families, and communities that will be affected by, and ideally benefit from, these services.

There are important cultural factors that play into how and when individuals may access mental health services. These include but are not limited to race, ethnicity, socioeconomic status, gender, sexual orientation, and religion. A skilled school mental health professional will take into consideration and adjust to the cultural norms of the student and family when providing school mental health service. These providers will need to seek out and increase their knowledge of various cultures while being careful to avoid stereotyping. The SAMHSA-funded Mental Health Technology and Transfer Center Network provides a wide array of free or low-cost webinars, trainings, and resources on equitable and inclusive interventions and supports for diverse populations for school and community-based mental health providers across the country (https://mhttcnetwork.org).

It is important for all staff in a school that wishes to implement school mental health services well to continually examine their own views, identities, and biases and to explore how these cultural factors may affect the development and delivery of school mental health services. Even within one school district, each school may serve a unique group of students and families. Adjust your plan as needed for each school's community.

SMALL STEPS DISTRICT AND SCHOOL LEADERS CAN TAKE IMMEDIATELY

While building robust systems of mental health supports in schools will take time, there are some initial steps that district and school leaders can do immediately to bring in more protective factors to schools. Building a strong tier 1 foundation in an MTSS using PBIS, social-emotional learning (SEL), and restorative justice practices can create a predictable, consistent, and safe learning environment for all students, which helps reduce stress and anxiety for students and staff. As mentioned earlier in this chapter, a stable and safe learning environment signals to a child's brain that it does not need to be on high alert and the brain can be more ready to learn and develop (McEwan, 2016).

The CDC's *What Works in Schools* initiative (2023) also recommends these initial steps in implementing SMH services:

- Increase school connectedness activities across all grades and for all youth.
- Connect families to community based mental health resources.
- Implement quality health education for all grades.

Schools can learn more about each of these recommendations by visiting the What Works in Schools website.

Increasing school connectedness, which was also highlighted in the chapter on restorative justice practices (chapter 5), is a powerful tier 1 strategy, and there are many simple, no-cost actions to implement to increase connections school-wide. Here are a few suggestions:

- Greet students at the door each day.
- Learn about students' sociocultural identity.
- Get to know your students' interests and likes by using daily connection questions.
- Have weekly or even daily check-ins with students.
- Strive to connect students' interests and academic content.

These connections can be built using community circles, journals, interest surveys, games, listening sessions, and making time for short conversations with students. It should be noted that increasing positive relationships and school connectedness is also an essential foundation of tier 2 and tier 3 supports that will be built as part of MTSS.

EXAMPLE FROM THE FIELD

Like many districts, the Kent School District in Kent, Washington increased their emphasis on wellness and mental health prevention and intervention activities when the COVID-19 pandemic began. As a midsized urban school district that is highly diverse and spans 73 square miles to serve 12 cities, the Kent School District witnesses a variety of mental health needs. The MTSS District Leadership Team that supports social, emotional, and behavioral needs knows the importance of building protective factors.

Two practices designed to facilitate connectedness that began during the pandemic are "Tell Me Tuesdays and Wellness Wednesdays." On Tell Me Tuesdays, the teachers do a check-in with the students to see how they are doing socially and emotionally through an online survey that only the teacher can see. They can also request to meet with another adult if desired. Wellness Wednesdays focus on small wellness-related steps that both students and staff can take, such as walking, deep breathing, or drinking more water. Kent also created individual calming bags with small comfort items for students to use when they became stressed during the pandemic.

REFERENCES

Barrett S., Eber, L., Perales, K., & Pohlman, K. (2021). *Fact Sheet Interconnected Systems Framework 101: An Introduction.* OSEP Technical Assistance Center on PBIS. www.pbis.org.

Center on the Developing Child. (2023). *The impact of early adversity on children's development.* Harvard University. https://developingchild.harvard.edu.

Centers for Disease Control and Prevention. (2017). *Youth risk behavior survey: Data summary and trends report.* www.cdc.gov/mmwr/volumes/67/ss/ss6708a1.htm.

Centers for Disease Control and Prevention. (2021). *Youth risk behavior survey: Data summary and trends report.* www.cdc.gov/healthyyouth/data/yrbs/pdf/YRBS_Data -Summary Trends_Report2023_508.pdf.

Centers for Disease Control and Prevention. (2023). *Youth risk behavior survey system.* https://www.cdc.gov/healthyyouth/data/yrbs/results.htm.

Colizzi, M., Lasalvia, A., & Ruggeri, M. (2020). Prevention and early intervention in youth mental health: Is it time for a multidisciplinary and trans-diagnostic model for care? *International Journal of Mental Health Systems, 14*, 23.

Eber, L., Barrett, S., Perales, K., Jeffrey-Pearsall, J., Pohlman, K., Putnam, R., Splett, J., & Weist, M. D. (2019). *Advancing education effectiveness: Interconnecting school mental health and school wide PBIS, Volume 2: An implementation guide.* Center for Positive Behavioral Interventions and Supports (funded by the Office of Special Education Programs, U.S. Department of Education). University of Oregon Press.

Flaherty, L. T., & Osher, D. (2003). History of school-based mental health services in the United States. In M. D. Weist, S. W. Evans, & N. A. Lever (eds.), *Handbook of school mental health: Advancing practice and research* (pp. 11–22). Kluwer Academic/Plenum Publishers.

McEwan, B. S. (2016). In pursuit of resilience: Stress, epigenetics, and brain plasticity. *Annals of the New York Academy of Science, 1373*: 56–64.

Mojtabai, R., & Olfson, M. (2020). National trends in mental health care for US adolescents. *JAMA Psychiatry.77*(7):703–714. doi: 10.1001/jamapsychiatry.2020.0279

Office of Elementary and Secondary Education. (2020). *Elementary and secondary school emergency relief fund.* https://oese.ed.gov/offices/education-stabilization -fund/elementary-secondary-school-emergency-relief-fund.

Skiba, R. J. (2015). Interventions to address racial/ethnic disparities in school discipline: Can systems reform be race-neutral? In R. Bangs & L. E. Davis (eds.), *Race and social problems* (pp. 107–124). Springer.

Splett, J. W., Perales, K., & Weist, M. D. (2019). *Interconnected systems framework— Implementation inventory (ISF-II), Version 3.* Unpublished instrument. Gainesville, FL: University of Florida.

Tobler, A. L, Maldonado-Molina, M. M., Staras, S. A. S., O'Mara, R. J., Livingston, M. D., & Komro, K. A. (2013). Perceived racial/ethnic discrimination, problem behaviors, and mental health among minority urban youth. *Ethnicity & Health, 18*(4), 337–349.

U.S. Department of Education, Office of Special Education and Rehabilitative Services. (2021). *Supporting child and student social, emotional, behavioral, and mental health needs.* Washington, DC.

U.S. Department of Education, Institute of Educational Sciences, School Pulse Panel. (2023). https://ies.ed.gov/schoolsurvey/spp.

White House. (2013). *Now Is the Time Initiative: The president's plan to protect our children and our communities by reducing gun violence.* https://obamawhitehouse .archives.gov/issues/preventing-gun-violence.

Chapter 7

Equity and Wellness in MTSS for Academics

WHAT DOES MTSS FOR ACADEMICS LOOK LIKE?

MTSS for academics is about providing all students high-quality instruction across the tiers that is matched to student's instructional needs and can be differentiated to better serve diverse learners. The instructional materials that staff use should reflect the racial and cultural diversity of the community they serve. This goes beyond just adding diverse books to the library or pictures of diverse leaders and influencers to the classroom walls.

Culturally responsive MTSS involves integrating the values and interests of students into the framework and understanding the ways that students may traditionally learn in their various cultural groups. These ways of learning may include rhythm, movement, singing, choral response, and time to be reflective. The best way to understand these needs is to get to know your students and their families.

Well-rounded instruction also integrates social-emotional learning opportunities into academics. Students' progress is frequently monitored and instructional content and teaching methods are adjusted according to this outcomes data (Fuchs & Fuchs, 2006). Just like any part of our MTSS framework, building a strong tier 1 core for academics is foundational.

At tier 2, educators provide instruction to students who are not making adequate gains by engaging them in small groups of four to six students. The core academic work is still the focus, but it is scaffolded based on the needs of the small group. This small group instruction should be occurring at least three times per week. Progress should be monitored at least bi-monthly in tier 2 to help scaffold the work on an ongoing basis.

Some students who are above grade level in their learning may also need tier 2 to offer more academic challenges and enrichment. Intervention groups and enrichment can occur in small groups right in the classroom. In some schools, tier 2 supports are offered when all students meet in group-based learning instruction. Many schools now use What I Need (WIN) groups. All students are placed in groups according to their current learning needs. These groups are often changed every six to eight weeks as needed, based on progress monitoring data.

Staff trained in MTSS tier 2 instruction offer structured instructional support to the small groups, which usually takes place in the classroom. Using this type of format keeps students from being pulled out of class for additional support. Pulling certain students out of class often occurs when other students in the class are receiving instruction in another topic; the students who have been pulled out of class miss that instruction in order to receive the support. Within these small groups, it is critical that staff are still mindful of the learning styles of their diverse learners.

At tier 3, a school continues to individualize students' learning needs in smaller groups of one to three students. The core instruction is made accessible through increased and intensive scaffolds based on the individual needs and skill gaps. One-on-one tutoring and instructional support may be provided. Some students with needs for tier 3 support may also benefit from the implementation of a 504 plan, which can provide additional accommodations. These accommodations might include special writing utensils, recorded lectures and books, or receiving handouts in advance.

At each tier of support, educators should strive to provide a culturally responsive education with the goal of moving the child back to tier 1. As students meet the academic benchmarks, they should exit from the higher tiers of support. The academic expectations for any child should never be lowered. MTSS allows educators to maintain high expectations for all students, when matched with the needed support level to meet those expectations. MTSS is about the environmental and instructional shifts we make to better support students.

ACADEMICS OUTCOMES FOR BIPOC STUDENTS

Many of you reading this book are already aware of the disparate outcomes in our schools between BIPOC learners and their White peers. The way in which academic systems and supports are created to either promote or prevent equity dramatically affects the school climate and student outcomes. Schools have traditionally had many systems that favor the promotion of White norms and learning styles. Research has shown that BIPOC students have poorer outcomes relative to White and Asian students.

Although disparate outcomes had long been highlighted in research, the 1983 report *A Nation at Risk* made these outcomes widely known. The report showed that only 40% of minority students were functionally literate, which sparked a national debate and call to action. This call to action highlighted the need for significant change in schools regarding the teaching and learning of diverse students.

In the 2001 No Child Left Behind (NCLB) Act and the 2004 reauthorization of the Individuals with Disabilities Education Act (IDEA) the first language appears around evidenced-based instruction, using data for decision-making, and accountability that pave the way for the birth of response to intervention (RTI).

However, the creation of RTI and later the more encompassing MTSS model does little to affect change for many students unless culturally responsive pedagogical practices, relationships, and connections that promote belonging with students and families, and a focus on wellness are employed. Not only are we not addressing the issues, but as Hammond (2015) points out, "Many of our students enter school with small learning gaps, but as they progress through school, the gap between African American and Latino and White students grows because we don't use culturally responsive practices and teach them how to be independent learners" (p.15). Howard and Terry (2011) reported that student outcomes, graduation rates, and post-secondary learning rates increased when schools used culturally responsive practices.

Even with the launch of MTSS, there continues to be an opportunity gap that is widening in many areas of our nation. The National Assessment of Educational Progress (NAEP) report for 2022 indicated that while all student groups when viewed by race made some gains compared to data from 1992, the gains are minimal and disparities between the learning outcomes of diverse learners and their White peers was still present. Additionally, the declines in learning attributed to the COVID-19 pandemic were more significant for students who reported lower access to teacher support and lacking access to technology and a quiet place to learn.

In addition to these gaps, the curriculum programs that a school chooses to use are often developed based on White values and learning styles. Our culturally diverse learners have been required to adapt to the dominant school culture (Boykin et al., 2005). This coupled with implicit biases and perceptions about our BIPOC students dramatically reduces the likely academic success of many students. These impacts can be ever-reaching, because research has shown that students with higher academic achievement are more likely to finish high school and succeed in post-secondary pursuits (Joppke & Morawska, 2003).

CORRELATION BETWEEN ACADEMIC
AND BEHAVIORAL OUTCOMES

Educators know that a relationship exists between academic performance and social, emotional, and behavioral health (Gray et al., 2014). Understanding this is key if their intent is to focus on the wellness in schools. Research has shown that students who start off with lagging skills in academics are more likely to have deficits in social skills, and the reverse is also true. A student who may initially lag behind peers in social skills is also more likely to show deficits in academic performance as they move through their time in school (Gray et al., 2014; Salla et al., 2016).

Research shows the strongest correlation between literacy skills and externalizing behaviors (Brennan et al., 2012). It makes sense that students who have trouble accessing the literacy content may develop behaviors from frustration or boredom and that children who have behavioral issues may miss instruction. One of the earliest studies that examined this correlation was done in 1984 by Coie and Krehbiel, who hypothesized four pathways that could explain this connection:

1. Behavior challenges reduce a child's access to academic instruction.
2. Attention deficits create lags in both academic and social skills.
3. Academic challenges lead to social rejection from peers or teachers.
4. Academic challenges lead the student to react with behavioral issues.

The outcomes of these pathways have been further validated with research and have been termed as crossover effects. While research shows some strong evidence that addressing academics will also positively impact behavior and vice versa, McIntosh and Goodman (2016) stress that these effects cannot be automatically assumed since some research shows a lack of impact when addressing only one area (Barton-Arwood et al., 2005). Since these pathways tend to only worsen the academic and behavioral outcomes across time, we can see the strong argument for early prevention and intervention work at tiers 1 and 2.

THE BENEFITS OF USING AN MTSS
FRAMEWORK FOR ACADEMICS

Prior to the intervention model, which was the foundational multi-tiered system focusing on academics, educators used what many deemed as a "wait and fail" model. This meant that when students failed to meet the academic benchmarks and fell two standard deviations below on standardized cognitive ability tests, they were quickly referred for special education. Unlike this model, the MTSS framework, when implemented with a lens on equity, causes educators to examine the cultural context of students and educators methods of teaching that may be affecting a student's learning.

This is a shift that has schools ask, "What about the environment or instruction is impacting this youth's ability to learn?" instead of focusing solely on the child as the problem. Focusing on culturally responsive teaching within a three-tiered model of support paired with the use of evidenced-based practices helps educators better meet the needs of all learners.

Culturally responsive teaching recognizes that students from diverse backgrounds bring with them a culture that is rich in traditions, where their language is an asset, and the home environment is important. Culturally responsive pedagogy shows us that to transform learning we have to transform the school. Hammond (2015) states that "culturally responsive teaching is one of the most powerful tools for helping students find their way out of the achievement gap."

Educators should always strive to hold high expectations for each and every student, so when a child struggles, they don't lower their expectations, but instead raise needed supports. Howard illustrates this further as he talks about how educators have to have empathy not sympathy in table 7.1 from his 2015 book *Why Race and Culture Matters in Schools*.

THE ROLE OF THE LEADER

Using an equity-based MTSS framework focused on wellness and positive school climate helps educators to dig into these oppressive systems and

Table 7.1. Why Race and Culture Matters in Schools.

Sympathetic Educators	Empathetic Educators
• Lower expectations of students due to race poverty or language • See limitations in students • See deficits in students • Have narrow, limited teaching repertoire due to perceived student capacity • Place little to no value on students' perspectives or voices • View learning as a teacher-dominated practice with students having little to offer • Feel sorry for students and enable failure to be commonplace for students	• Hold students accountable despite difficult circumstances • See promise and possibility in students • See assets in students • Become active problem solvers • Develop critical and complex teaching practices to engage students • Listen and learn from students' experiences to inform teaching • View learning as a reciprocal process between teacher and student • Tap into students' cultural capital as a means to teaching and learning

Characteristics of sympathetic vs. empathetic teachers from Howard, T. (2015.)

beliefs and create schools where all students can thrive academically. Howard (2020) writes:

> the vision of school transformation by leaders is clearly articulated to anyone inquiring about the mission of the school, the goals for the given school year, and in the school's list of top priorities. These leaders set a tone and vision of high achievement, work tirelessly to ensure academic success for all students, and were relentless in their efforts to get all stakeholders to buy into the vision for student learning.

Hollins-Sims et al. (2023) suggest that schools focus first on growing staff self-awareness around the implicit thoughts, feelings and behaviors that exist about diverse students and then do this same examination about the system. This, of course, is no simple undertaking but can help educators examine school systems from an academic perspective.

A district or school's academic data can help shed light on which students are being successful. Teams must then examine the curriculum and teaching strategies to assess if it is culturally responsive for the students being served. Williams (2015) remind us that schools must go beyond just awareness and must understand the cultural characteristics of the students they serve, and the backgrounds and values of the students and their families.

Once schools and educators know their students' backgrounds and values, they can use this information to create culturally relevant instruction. Students will truly feel seen, heard, and valued when their educators have created a culturally affirming school. There is a growing body of research that shows when cultural characteristics that students identify with are incorporated into the classroom, the academic engagement of students can greatly increase (Allen & Boynkin, 1991; Carter, et al., 2008). A culturally relevant MTSS framework places the interests, values, and cultural identities of students at the center of instruction and problem-solving.

Leaders must ensure that staff have the permission and time to get to know the interests and cultures of the students and families so that relationships can be built and a culture of belonging can be a central focus in their schools. Since the COVID-19 pandemic, pressure to focus on academic recovery has run high and some schools have set aside the time for connection to solely focus on the academics. Greenwood et al. (1994) note that engagement was the best mediating variable between instruction and academic achievement. Remember that MTSS is your own recipe that must be adjusted for your school or district.

While there are many aspects to leadership within an MTSS framework, the importance of team structures and practices and the use of data for decision-making will be highlighted here. These two aspects are key to creating a high functioning system within an MTTS.

THE ROLE OF TEAMING IN ACADEMIC MTSS

If you have read the prior chapters, it should be no surprise that developing a strong MTSS for academics starts with a leadership team. Your tier 1 team focused on academic supports can also focus on behavior but may need to meet more frequently and intentionally schedule when behavior vs. academic discussions will occur. In some schools, especially smaller elementary schools, the same team meets weekly and rotates talking about behavior needs one week and academic needs the next week. It is important that these meetings have the team roles, agenda, and note-taking processes discussed in chapter 1.

One of the main roles of this team is to implement the school's implementation plan for the instructional components of MTSS. Because this can feel like a daunting task, the instructional team may need to prioritize which instructional areas the team focuses on first. Team tasks may include:

- Creating and using a schoolwide implementation plan to drive the focus of this team
- Collaborating and supporting grade or content area teams or professional learning communities
- Assessing the core tier 1 instructional methods and routines
- Creating benchmark data assessment schedules
- Obtaining needed professional development and coaching for staff
- Arranging for family and community partnerships with the school that includes shared decision-making

Because making database decisions is a major undertaking, the team must also adopt a consistent procedure and routine for this. Specific types of decisions such as how to form and adjust instructional groups should happen on a schedule so that students are receiving support that is targeted for their current needs. For elementary schools, student academic groups can be reviewed every six weeks and adjusted as students move up in their skill level. This review may be done in grade-level teams or professional learning communities or by the building level teams. These discussions should occur immediately following benchmark data collection.

USING DATA TO GUIDE DECISION-MAKING
AND ENSURE EQUITY

Data is also a powerful tool to ensure that all our students are meeting equitable academic outcomes. The data in MTSS should integrate the academic and behavioral data as much as possible. This integration can be accomplished by examining both the academic and behavioral data at the same time to consider if one outcome is causing or impacting another outcome. Educators can also run data by subgroups (e.g., race, ethnicity, gender, grade level) to check for disproportionality. Academic data comes in many forms, and it's important that teams use all the various forms discussed in the following paragraphs.

FIDELITY DATA IN MTSS FOR ACADEMICS

Fidelity tools help educators to answer the question "Are we doing what we said we would do?" or "Are we implementing the initiative or program the way in which it was intended to be implemented?" It's hard to complain that you are not getting the outcomes you hoped to see if the MTSS system is not being implemented with fidelity. Ideally, when using fidelity tools you start by gaining a baseline data point. This data point helps you assess what is already in place that can serve as the building blocks for the MTSS system. Baseline data also helps a school outline a plan or roadmap for their implementation.

To date, there is a lack of fidelity tools related to implementation of academic efforts. Two tools that can help schools to examine their implementation of reading are the *Planning and Evaluation Tool for Effective Schoolwide Reading Programs* (PET-R) (Kame'enui & Simmons, 2002) and the *Reading Tiered Fidelity Inventory* (R-TFI V2) (St. Martin et al., 2022). Both tools are free for schools and districts to use.

The PET-R is a yearly self-assessment designed to be completed by members of the MTSS team that measures the overall implementation of reading for your school. The R-TFI is also designed for teams to self-assess reading yearly. It breaks down implementation into tier 1 universal reading implementation and an advanced tiers inventory to measure implementation of support for tiers 2 and 3. The R-TFI has a reporting system in which scores can be entered and graphed to track growth over time. Fidelity should also be measured by the various curriculum or interventions that a school implements. The following sample questions are organized by tool.

PET-R (2017) sample questions:

- Teachers and instructional staff have a thorough understanding and working knowledge of grade-level instructional/reading priorities and effective practices.
- Professional development efforts are explicitly linked to practices and programs that have been shown to be effective through documented research.
- Administrators or the leadership team are knowledgeable of state standards, priority reading skills and strategies, assessment measures and practices, and instructional programs and materials.

R-TFI (Secondary Edition, 2022) sample questions:

- The school leadership team supports the implementation of the tier 1 adolescent literacy components of an MTSS framework.
- The school has a comprehensive tier 1 assessment system and personnel to support the system.
- The principal(s) and teachers access ongoing professional learning in practices that support adolescent literacy in an MTSS framework.

Once schools have completed the yearly fidelity assessment and action planning, they can continue to monitor the progress with these same tools.

FORMATIVE AND SUMMATIVE DATA IN MTSS FOR ACADEMICS

Formative data is collected periodically as a student is learning new information. Curriculum-based measures (CBMs) are brief assessments of the core skills that are implemented frequently (Deno & Mirkin, 1977). These measures usually require only one to three minutes to administer and allow a teacher to gauge if the student is making growth in a skill area. CBMs are highly sensitive to student growth and can detect small changes in a student's academic performance (Deno et al., 2001). Each student's individual performance can then be compared to their own performance over time as well as compared to peers in the same grade.

The summative assessments are generally administered at the end of a unit or grading period and summarize what students have learned. There are several commercial databases that allow educators to capture and use formative and summative assessments. Examples include Easy CBM (www.easycbm.com) and Aims Webb (www.aimsweb.com).

These formative and summative assessments can also serve as diagnostic assessments that allow you to more clearly assess the exact nature of students' needs so that you can most effectively and efficiently provide the targeted group and individual supports. A diagnostic assessment that is familiar to many schools and can also be used as a formative curriculum-based measure is the Dynamic Indicators of Basic Early Literacy Skills (DIBELS 8) (University of Oregon, 2023).

GENERAL OUTCOMES DATA IN MTSS FOR ACADEMICS

General outcome measures allow you to see that you are making the higher-level gains you want to see for both academics and behavioral or social-emotional supports. These outcome measures should be viewed at least yearly, but are often examined monthly. Examples of general outcomes data are office discipline referrals, suspension and expulsion data, absentee and truancy data, and whether students are meeting yearly academic benchmarks on standardized testing. All data should also be viewed for equity by running the data to look for any disproportionality among subgroups of students and families.

PERCEPTIONS DATA IN MTSS FOR ACADEMICS

Use of perceptions data is growing among schools and districts. Perceptions data provides you with an important perspective about how our efforts are truly benefiting and impacting the students and families we serve. Perceptions data involves gathering opinions, feedback, and recommendations about your school and programs from are invested parties. Perceptions data can be captured through surveys, focus groups, interviews and open-ended written answers to questions.

In *Street Data,* Safir and Dugan (2021) discuss gathering perceptions data that focuses on what is going right with our students and communities and talking a strengths-based approach to capitalize on what's working instead of only trying to fix what is not working.

Perceptions data in schools can be gathered from a variety of our invested parties which may include:

- Students
- Families
- School staff
- School administrators
- School board members

- Community members
- Collaborating partners (after-school programs, public library, youth agencies)
- Other interested parties

The intent of this data is to really gauge if your work is making a positive change to your school climate and helps to determine where you spend your time and energy. Assuring that what school leaders and staff see as important also matches with what your invested parties see as important can help drive the buy-in needed for change.

HOW TO GET STARTED

School leaders should use their data to help inform the right place to start. If you haven't already, form a team that can look at and/or collect data that can help inform where to invest your time. Many schools start with looking at academic data related to reading since reading has impacts across the content areas. Investing in high-quality training and coaching supports will help your team create an implementation plan and access the needed professional development for your school or district.

Applying the implementation science logic will also help to ensure that you create a framework that is both effective and sustainable. Table 7.2 can guide you to use the implementation science framework for academics in MTSS.

EXAMPLE FROM THE FIELD

The Kent School District in Kent, Washington had been focusing their MTSS work on building needed social-emotional and behavioral supports for six years when they also began to build out an MTSS focusing on reading. They had focused initially on behavior, knowing that behavior was interfering with learning and instruction. One of the first steps for increasing their focus on reading was to get a baseline of the fidelity of reading instruction in all 43 schools, using the R-TFI. Simultaneously, the schools began a process to map out the current reading curriculum being used in tier 1 and what they were already doing to support students who needed more beyond tier 1.

Like many districts getting started with this work specific to reading, Kent found schools that already had many of the indicators of the R-TFI fully in place and others in the beginning stages. They noticed that some of the greatest need was providing the secondary schools with reading strategies that could be infused across all content areas pushed out by the department chairs.

Table 7.2. Stages of Implementation Applied to School Mental Health and the Interconnected Schools Framework

Implementation Stages	School Mental Health Application
Exploration—Identify the need for change, compare possible approaches to achieve change, and assess readiness for change.	Have we used a needs assessment to clearly identify what the need is related to MTSS for academics? What academics supports are in place now in each tier? What is our current level of readiness for change? Do we have a representative team in place to guide this work?
Installation—Identify the needed supports to put the practice in place with good fidelity. Gather feedback from those who will be affected.	What are the systems that need to be built to ensure that the academic core can be implemented with high fidelity? What needs to be installed to bring in tier 2 and tier 3 supports for academics? What measurable outcomes goals have been identified?
Initial Implementation—Initial training and coaching and data review supports the new skills and practices, and improvement in implementation.	Academic practices are adopted into and aligned with the larger MTSS framework within the school. Staff members are trained in the needed academic strategies and related curriculum and are actively engaged in the implementation. There is clear communication about the integration of academics and social, emotional, and behavioral learning with families and students. Assessment of the fidelity of implementation and collection of related outcomes data is ongoing.
Full Implementation—The innovation is well-integrated into the daily practice and routines. It remains in place through administrative changes.	All staff know their role in implementing academic supports. New academic practices are integrated into the policies and procedures. Funding to maintain a high level of academic supports is secured.

Overall, the schools found the R-TFI to be a useful tool in helping them create an action plan focused on reading instruction.

REFERENCES

Allen, B. A., & Wade Boykin, W. (1991). The influence of contextual factors on Afro American and Euro-American children's performance: Effects of movement opportunity 2nd music, *International Journal of Psychology, 26*, 373–387.

Barton-Arwood, S. M., Wehby, J. H., & Falk, K. B. (2005). Reading instruction for elementary-age students with emotional and behavioral disorders: Academic and behavioral outcomes. *Exceptional Children, 72*, 7–27.

Boykin, A. W., Albury, A., Tyler, K. M., Hurley, E. A., Bailey, C. T., & Miller, O. A. (2005). The influence of culture on the perceptions of academic achievement among low-income African and Anglo American elementary students. *Cultural Diversity and Ethnic Minority Psychology, 11*(4), 339–350.

Brennan, L. M., Shaw, D. S., Dishion, T. J., & Wilson, M. (2012). Longitudinal predictors of school-age academic achievement: Unique contributions of toddler-age aggression, oppositionality, inattention, and hyperactivity. *Journal of Abnormal Child Psychology, 40*, 1289–1300.

Carter, N. C., Hawkins, T. N., & Natesan, P. (2008). The relationship between verve and the academic achievement African American students in reading and mathematics in an urban middle school. *Educational Foundations*, 29–46.

Coie, J. D., & Krehbiel, G. (1984). Effects of academic tutoring on the social status of low achieving, socially rejected children. *Child Development, 55*, 1465–1478.

Deno, S., Fuchs, L. S., Martson, D., & Shin, J. (2001). Using curriculum-based measurements to establish growth standards for students with learning disabilities. *School Psychology Review, 30*, 507–524.

Deno S. L., & Mirkin, P. K. (1977). Data-based program modification: A manual. Council for Exceptional Children.

Fuchs, D., & Fuchs, L. (2006). Introduction to response to Intervention: What, why and how valid is it? *Reading Research Quarterly, 41*, 93–99.

Gray, S. A., Carter, A. S., Briggs-Gowan, M. J., Jones, S. M., & Wagmiller, R. L. (2014). Growth trajectories of early aggression, overactivity and inattention: Relations to second-grade reading. *Developmental Psychology, 50*, 2255–2263.

Greenwood, C. R., Terry, B., Marquis, J., & Walker, D. (1994). Confirming a performance-based instructional model. *School Psychology Review, 23*, 652–681.

Hammond, Z. (2015). *Culturally responsive teaching and the brain: Promoting authentic engagement and rigor among children and linguistically diverse students*. Corwin Publishing.

Howard, T. (2010). *Why race and culture matter in schools: Closing the achievement gap in America's classrooms.* Teachers College Press.

Howard, T. C., & Terry, C. L. (2011). Culturally responsive pedagogy for African American students: Promising programs and practices for enhanced academic performance. *Teaching Education 22*, 345–362.

Joppke, C., & Morawska, E. T. (2003). *Toward assimilation and citizenship: Immigrants in liberal nation-states*. Palgrave Macmillan.

Kame'enui, E. J. Simmons, D. C. (2003). *Planning and Evaluation Tool for Effective Schoolwide Reading Programs—Revised (PET-R)*. University of Oregon.

McIntosh, K., & Goodman, S. (2016). *Integrated multi-tiered systems of support.* Guilford Press.

Mellard, D. F., & Johnson, E. S. (2008). Response to Intervention: A practitioner's guide to implementation. Corwin Press.

National assessment of educational progress report card. (2022). https://www.nationsreportcard.gov.

Safir, S., & Dugan, J. (2021). *Street data: A next-generation model for equity, pedagogy, and school transformation.* Corwin Publishing.

Salla, J., Michel, G., Pingault, J. B., Lacourse, E., Paquin, S., Galéra, C., Falissard, B., Boivin, M., Tremblay, R. E., & Côté, S. M. (2016). Childhood trajectories of inattention-hyperactivity and academic achievement at 12 years. *European Child & Adolescent Psychiatry, 25,* 1195–1206.

St. Martin, K., Harms, A., Walsh, M., & Nantais, M. (2022). *Reading tiered fidelity inventory elementary-level edition.* (Version 2.0). Michigan Department of Education, Michigan's Multi-Tiered System of Supports Technical Assistance Center.

University of Oregon. (2023). *8th Edition of dynamic indicators of basic early literacy skills (DIBELS®): Administration and scoring guide, 2023 edition.* Eugene: University of Oregon. https://dibels.uoregon.edu.

Williams, D. D. (2015). *An RTI guide to improving the performance of African American children.* Corwin Publishing.

Chapter 8

Putting It All Together

Building a comprehensive MTSS framework is a significant undertaking, but has great benefits for schools and communities. The ability to create efficient and effective systems that allow students, families, and staff to access increased services and support in an equitable and timely manner benefits everyone. The best outcomes arise when we hold true to what we value and combine that with the key ingredients in our MTSS recipe. As you grow in your implementation, you may find that you add in more ingredients to that recipe and, over time, it uniquely reflects your school community.

RETURNING TO THE RECIPE

As the introduction noted, the MTSS framework can define the benchmarks, tools, and skills needed to effectively implement it. By meaningfully involving all members of the community in the development of a shared, inclusive school community, all members of the community feel seen, welcomed, and included. When we use our four core MTSS ingredients of equity, connectedness, inclusivity, and culturally responsive pedagogy and combine those with the ingredients needed in our individual educational contexts, we can truly bring about systemic change. Remember, *you* are the best tool in your toolbox.

As McIntosh and Goodman (2016) note, "all change is difficult, even when we know that this change will lead to the improvement and outcomes we value." With ever-increasing demands on educators' and education leaders' time, we must be strategic about how we bring all the core initiatives together within the MTSS framework. Leaders need to give themselves permission to focus on doing a few things well and add on strategically.

ADVICE FROM THE FIELD

We close this book with advice from two of the leaders who provided examples for us in previous chapters. Cheri Simpson, director of Student and Family Support Services, from the Kent School District in Kent, Washington, said that after seven years of focusing on MTSS these are the factors she has found most impactful for building and sustaining MTSS.

- A superintendent who supports MTSS as one of their primary goals, and district leadership sharing that vision.
- A district-level MTSS team representative of the district, schools, families, and community who can support the MTSS directive.
- Using a yearly district-level fidelity tool to measure implementation.
- High visibility with all invested parties of the MTSS work.
- A relationships-first approach that takes the time needed to build up trust with all invested parties.
- The knowledge that we are constantly adapting to meet schools where they are; it can't be one size fits all.
- A team of skilled MTSS coaches that has high collaboration and weekly meetings.

Johnny Phu, director of Student Services in the Lake Washington School District in Redmond, Washington, has worked with multiple districts on MTSS and shared these factors for implementation and sustainability.

- Understand the history and strengths of the community your district serves.
- Map how the values of the community and those of the district align.
- Bring invested parties' (families, students, and community) voices to the MTSS process.
- Know that in a large district, the context and community values can change across schools, which is why MTSS is designed to be flexible.
- Set up tight systems around communication.
- Invest in your infrastructure for training and coaching.

One last time, we ask you, what is your recipe for implementation of MTSS in your school or district? What data are you using to make the MTSS framework equitable, inclusive, and culturally responsive? What strategic tools will assist you in the implementation of MTSS that is equitable, full of love, centered in evidence-based practice, and understands the history of its community and education? What first step are you ready to take?

FINAL THOUGHTS

With over 60 years of collective experience, we as the authors have seen a lot of fads, initiatives, and yes, even shocking things occur in education. None have held the promise that we feel MTSS has held to truly help us build the systems and supports our students, families, and educators need. The work of building schools that are both highly effective and efficient is definitely a daunting journey. We hope that this book can serve as a guide that you can use on that journey.

REFERENCE

McIntosh, K., & Goodman, S. (2016). *Integrated multi-tiered systems of support.* Guilford Press.

About the Authors

Dr. **Lori Lynass** has worked in the field of education since 1998. She began her career as a special education teacher and taught in a juvenile justice facility, a K–12 school, and a comprehensive middle school. Her teaching focused on serving students with learning disabilities and social, emotional, and behavioral support needs. She has also worked for the University of Washington as a Research Scientist managing large federal research and was the first executive director for the Northwest PBIS Network. She has taught courses for the University of Washington, Seattle University, and Seattle Pacific University as an adjunct professor. She has published articles on the topics of behavior, multi-tiered systems of support (MTSS), and restorative justice. She owns Sound Supports, a consulting company that has served over 2,000 schools, 200 school districts, and four state departments of education with their training, coaching, and evaluation needs related to MTSS, positive behavior intervention and supports (PBIS), special education, and restorative justice. She lives in Shoreline, Washington, with her husband, son, daughter, and lively Boston terrier.

Dr. **Erika L. McDowell** is a former New Jersey governor's award recipient and honors graduate of Howard University and New York University. She is an equity steward at Wildflower Schools, co-CEO of the Black Wildflower Fund, and owner of Inspired Minds Collide, LLC. She earned her EdD from Drexel University in Educational Leadership and Management in May 2020. Dr. McDowell has received the Association for Positive Behavior Support's 2020 E.G., "Ted" Carr Early Career Practitioner Award and has been elected to the Association for Positive Behavior Support board of directors for the 2021–2024 term, serving in the inaugural Racial and Ethnic Diversity Seat. Most recently, Dr. McDowell was honored as one of Drexel University's 40 under 40 in 2022. She has served as an executive director of professional development and director of PBIS/Youth Court for the School District of Philadelphia. Other previous positions include assistant principal and teacher. Her in-depth experience includes restorative practices, equity, positive behavioral support, conflict resolution, classroom management, coaching, leadership development, and behavioral data support. In June 2022, she began her appointment as a clinical associate professor of educational leadership and policy at the State University of New York at Buffalo. Dr. McDowell continues to be committed to nurturing the minds and gifts of leaders, teachers, and youth nationwide.

Dr. **Bridget Walker** has worked in education for over three decades, serving in a variety of direct service and leadership positions, including special education teacher for K–12 students with high incidence disabilities, day treatment program teacher, district behavior specialist, state PBIS project coordinator, school improvement coach, and teacher educator at the University of Washington and Seattle University. Dr. Walker has a private consulting practice supporting districts and schools in the areas of PBIS, MTSS, and developing equitable, inclusive, and effective trauma-informed and restorative practices for students with intensive learning and behavior challenges. Dr. Walker regularly provides professional development in building and sustaining tiered systems of supports, universal design of learning, social emotional learning, trauma-informed and restorative practices and other aspects of school and district transformation. She has published several journal articles, book chapters, and books related to tiered systems of support and developing effective services and supports for students with intensive learning and behavior challenges. In 2011, she was awarded the PBIS Champion award by the Northwest Positive Behavior Interventions and Supports Network for her ongoing work in helping schools effectively implement PBIS to support the success of *all* students.

Made in United States
Troutdale, OR
09/30/2024